Praise for
The Right Decision Every Time

"*The Right Decision Every Time* is a <u>wonderful</u> book and should be mandatory (and life-saving!) reading for every executive. The ability to quickly and effectively focus your mind on the subject at hand, independent of what is going on around you, is a critical skill that any leader has to master in order to excel. Most successful business people, myself included, pride themselves on their ability to 'multi-task' and accomplish large amounts of 'work' during the business day. This book made me realize that this very action has actually been a detriment to my assessing business goals and making more thoughtful or 'right' decisions. *The Right Decision Every Time* teaches us how to engage our subconscious at will, which enables us to make sound, clear decisions that are not in conflict with ourselves or our ultimate goal."

Debi Davis, CEO, Fit America

"Luda Kopeikina has provided a practical and much-needed framework that allows executives at all levels to improve their decision making. To improve your decision making—and results—read this book."

Michael Treacy, author of *Double-Digit Growth and The Discipline of Market Leaders*

"Wrong assumptions and incongruence of the team with the decision are among the main reasons for corporate failure. To avoid these dangerous wrong turns, every executive should study Luda Kopeikina's five-step process for making clear decisions."

Raymond P. Schiavone, President & CEO, Arbortext

"Leaders value decision clarity. Clear decisions are easier to communicate and they can be used as inspiring calls for action. A must-read book for any executive who wants to increase clarity in their decisions and excel in business."

E. Linn Draper, Jr., Retired Chairman, President, and Chief Executive Officer, American Electric Power

"This excellent book addresses a rarely discussed topic in business literature—the effect of emotions in decision-making and how to harness them for greater effectiveness. A practical and insightful book for all business leaders and managers on the art and science of making tough decisions."

Bruce Cryer, CEO, HeartMath, Author of *From Chaos to Coherence: The Power to Change Performance*

"Luda Kopeikina's decision-making process is innovative, just like she is. She asks a tough question: Is there a state of being that will enable leaders to make better decisions? Her excellent and well-researched approach shows that there is—a Clarity State. In this exciting and ground-breaking book, Luda shows us how to use this profound state to make better and clearer decisions when it really matters."

Cindy Kushner, President of Women Executive Leadership, Partner, KPMG

"*The Right Decision Every Time* presents real-life examples of tough, complex decisions faced by CEOs every day. It should be required reading for any executive, but especially the younger ones, striving to balance risk, success, and the emotional toll tough decisions take on us."

Chris Schuster, President and CEO, Emerson Hospital

"The success of a business is simply the sum total of all the decisions made. Kopeikina's book is the first to provide a practical approach to dramatically increase the speed and quality of decision-making in an organization. Nothing is more important than making the right decision."

Verne Harnish, CEO, Gazelles; Founder of YEO and author of *Mastering the Rockefeller Habits*

"Every executive aspiring to be a good leader should read this book. All of us strive to make better decisions. With experience we come to realize that what really matters is how we make those important decisions. This book takes the reader through thought provoking questions and allows reflection on previous decisions as an extremely useful learning process into the nature of your personal decision-making style. It also introduces a powerful framework for making better decisions. An important and extremely timely book."

Chiang Gnee HENG, Deputy President, Sembcorp Marine Limited, Singapore

"*The Right Decision Every Time* is a true eye-opening enabler for executives who have to make tough decisions in a fast-paced business environment. Luda Kopeikina's work on decision-making not only names the power behind good decisions—vision, personal commitment, and alignment of analytical and emotional capabilities—but also provides practical tools to unleash that power on critical decisions."

Katja von Raven, VP Marketing, Newell Rubbermaid

"Want to learn how to make better decisions—reliably? Read this book.

Luda Kopeikina shares lessons learned from her work with master decision makers Jack Welch of GE and Larry Bossidy of Allied Signal; from her personal experience as a highly successful CEO of a publicly traded technology firm; from interviews with over one hundred successful CEOs around the nation; and from academic research on decision making at MIT and other eminent universities. Her conclusion? The best decisions flow from a clear head, joined to a trained gut. She then lays out a coherent, step-by-step technique that anyone can follow, to make better decisions, each and every time.

The result is a system that unites rational analysis with a method for tapping into those deep intuitive powers of the mind, described in Malcolm Gladwell's *Blink*.

Highly recommended for all decision makers, and all those who aspire to be one."

Keith Collins, MD, CEO, PhyTrust

"Deeply-buried biases can lead us in the wrong direction. Uncovering decision biases is easier said than done. *The Right Decision Every Time* provides a coherent description of the state of clarity that can help anyone identify alternative decision perspectives and select the right one. This book is not just for business managers. Every one of us can use the insights and techniques presented in the book to eradicate doubts, stop wasting time in deciding and start acting!"

John Van Maanen, Erwin H. Schell Professor of Organization Studies, MIT

"Complex decisions often involve diverging opinions and team conflicts. It is the job of a leader to make a decision, unite the team, and lead the way to a successful implementation. *The Right Decision Every Time* addresses these challenges and provides practical techniques for resolving conflict and creating team unity. I am excited that this book can help anyone make clearer decisions in complex situations."

Adrienne Arsht, Chairman, TotalBank

"*The Right Decision Every Time* will make a tremendous difference in the effectiveness of those who adopt its message."

Carl A. Erikson, Energy and Management Consultant;
Former Senior Vice President, American Electric Power

"Every entrepreneur should read this book! Entrepreneurs face decisions that are not only complex, but are of the "make-or-break" kind. While in the midst of juggling myriad priorities, constraints, problems, and opportunities, it is challenging to clearly focus on crucial, strategic decisions. The Clarity State and the simple but powerful decision–making techniques described in the book work for me and will help anyone who is striving to reach clarity in a situation with little available, or conflicting data."

Cheryl L. Clarkson, Founder and CEO, SkinHealth

"*The Right Decision Every Time* delivers on its promise to help the reader reach perfect clarity on tough decisions. A comprehensive technique to decision-making that focuses your physical, mental, and emotional resources is taught and reinforced, with a wealth of examples where executives used the technique to actually make real decisions. Luda Kopeikina shows that reaching perfect clarity on tough decisions is a skill and that it can be learned. Luda has uncluttered the process of decision-making, and in doing so, she equips decision makers with the tools to make consistently better decisions.

As I read this book, several business decisions I am currently facing were seen in much better clarity. This book promises to change organizations and their cultures, both large and small, as a manual on how to achieve perfect clarity on tough decisions."

Anthony J. Ahern, President & CEO, Buckeye Power,
Ohio Rural Electric Cooperatives

"Luda Kopeikina has created an innovative approach to making effective decisions quickly. *The Right Decision Every Time* provides you with a process, or a decision map, to follow, guiding you to solutions which you can implement with conviction. It is an easy, straightforward, but powerful process. Any leader would do well by adopting this approach, particularly when faced with complex, challenging decisions that can leave an organization in limbo until they are resolved."

R. Jeffrey Bailly, President & CEO, UFP Technologies

"Our ability to generate sustainable shareholder value depends on our capacity to make the right decision every time. Luda Kopeikina introduces a practical framework for weeding out clutter and preparing the ground for thoughtful decisions. Full of telling insights, her book is a pleasure to read."

James J. Schiro, Chief Executive Officer, Zurich Financial Services

The Right Decision Every Time

How to Reach
Perfect Clarity on Tough Decisions

Luda Kopeikina

PEARSON

Prentice
Hall

Upper Saddle River, NJ • New York • San Francisco • Toronto
London • Munich • Paris • Madrid
Capetown • Sydney • Tokyo • Singapore • Mexico City

Library of Congress Catalog Number: 2005923710

Vice President and Editor-in-Chief: Tim Moore
Acquisitions Editor: Paula Sinnott
Editorial Assistant: Susie Abraham
Development Editor: Russ Hall
Marketing Manager: John Pierce
International Marketing Manager: Tim Galligan
Cover Designer: Solid State Graphics
Managing Editor: Gina Kanouse
Project Editor: Rose Sweazy
Copy Editor: Ben Lawson
Senior Indexer: Cheryl Lenser
Senior Compositor: Gloria Schurick
Manufacturing Buyer: Dan Uhrig

©2005 by Pearson Education, Inc.
Publishing as Prentice Hall
Upper Saddle River, New Jersey 07458

Prentice Hall offers excellent discounts on this book when ordered in quantity for bulk purchases or special sales. For more information, please contact U.S. Corporate and Government Sales, 1-800-382-3419, corpsales@pearsontechgroup.com. For sales outside the U.S., please contact International Sales, 1-317-581-3793, international@pearsontechgroup.com.

Printed in the United States of America

Second Printing, September 2005

ISBN 0-131-86262-6
Pearson Education LTD.
Pearson Education Australia PTY, Limited.
Pearson Education Singapore, Pte. Ltd.
Pearson Education North Asia, Ltd.
Pearson Education Canada, Ltd.
Pearson Educatión de Mexico, S.A. de C.V.
Pearson Education—Japan
Pearson Education Malaysia, Pte. Ltd.

To Igor, whose support and encouragement enabled me to become the person I am.

Contents

Acknowledgments

First there was a fascinating question that I was always deeply interested in answering—"How does your state of being influence your decisions?", and then a research project at the MIT Sloan School of Management, and then this book based on that research. Four people stand at the root of the research project and thus this book. Without them, the book would not have happened. My husband told me to "follow my gut" when the project was just a vague and rather far-fetched idea. Alan White, Senior Associate Dean of the MIT Sloan School of Management, became a cornerstone in making it a reality. My sincere gratitude also goes to Ed Schein, MIT Sloan Fellows Professor of Management, Emeritus, whose tremendous wisdom helped me reveal directions, focus, question, and structure approaches, and John Van Maanen, MIT Sloan Professor of Organizational Studies, whose boundless positive energy, can-do attitude, innate curiosity, and unusual approaches helped me probe the subject from a wide variety of angles.

When the work shaped into a book, there were a number of people without whom the book would not have been published. Ed Roberts, MIT Sloan Professor of the Management of Technology, the ever-present influence in my life, sent me in the right direction; Michael Treacy, the author of two best-selling books on management, provided guidance and contacts; Helen Rees, my literary agent, found the right publisher; and Paula Sinnott, an action-oriented, full-of-upbeat-energy editor at Prentice Hall, managed the book's birth.

I feel honored to have these wonderful people in my life and to have had the opportunity to work with them.

In search for answers to my questions, I turned to CEOs—a group of people with the toughest job in the business world. I am sincerely grateful to numerous CEOs who shared their thoughts about this intriguing topic and worked with me on their decisions in order to refine the process presented in the book. It was truly a collaborative effort! The examples in this book are true stories taken from my work with them.

Special thanks go to Carl Erikson, who has a unique talent of knowing how to say the right things at the right time and who also suffered through the first draft of the book; Linn Draper, former CEO of AEP, who, despite an enormous load and busy schedule, dedicated time to try the process and comment on it; Mike Armstrong, former CEO of AT&T, who listened to the concepts and, with his wise council, encouraged me to proceed; Cheryl Clarkson and Jeff Bailly, who were in the first group of courageous CEOs willing to try the process on their decisions; Verne Harnish, whose endless energy and connections were helpful in recruiting entrepreneurial CEOs to participate in the project; and the Sloan Fellows class of 2004, who tested the first, "raw" version of the process.

Truth be known, nothing can be created without love and support. My wonderful family, Igor and Kathy, thank you for providing this in abundance—I always feel special because of your presence in my life.

About the Author

Luda Kopeikina is a Visiting Scholar at the MIT Sloan School of Management and CEO of Noventra Corporation, an innovation commercialization firm. Ms. Kopeikina spent six years at General Electric in various vice presidential positions, where she had an opportunity to work with Jack Welch and observe his methods in action. Later she was President and CEO of Celerity Solutions, Inc., a publicly traded company. Under her leadership, the company executed a complete turnaround in two years and grew six-fold. Interactive Week's 1998 Executive Worth Survey ranked Ms. Kopeikina within the top 20 CEOs of U.S. high-tech public companies for her performance and total return to shareholders.

Ms. Kopeikina is an entrepreneur who started two successful companies. She enjoys working with entrepreneurs and helping businesses prosper. She is a Chairman of MIT Enterprise Forum of South Florida, a nonprofit organization that promotes entrepreneurship. She also serves on the Board of Directors of several companies.

Ms. Kopeikina holds a master's degree from MIT's Sloan School of Management as a Sloan Fellow. She also holds a master's degree in computer science from St. Petersburg University, Russia, where she completed a Ph.D. thesis in computer science.

For additional information about the book and the author, or to share your experiences in clear decision-making with the author, please visit www.ludakopeikina.com

Introduction

I first became interested in the link between the state of mind and effective decision-making early in my life when I faced a personal tough choice of leaving the Soviet Union in the early 1980s. The question was whether I was willing to abandon my comfortable life, a high-level position at the top university, and leave the country alone, pregnant, with only ninety dollars in my pocket and forty pounds of luggage, or to stay and "act within the limits" imposed by the regime.

I wondered then why some decisions are more difficult than others and how people make such tough choices effectively. Is there a state of mind that enables us to make tough decisions easier? I questioned. Through my executive career, I watched master decision makers whom I chanced to meet, especially at General Electric, where I was privileged to become a VP, eager to learn more about the link between the state of mind and effective decision-making. It became clear to me that behind their mastery and ease of making decisions is a discipline, a method, and much introspection and self-improvement that are not visible to the naked eye.

Since then, I studied mind-focusing methods more systematically and applied them to my decision-making as a CEO of a public and then a private company. Research for this book served as a culmination of the exploration into this topic. I worked with over 100 CEO's from companies of various sizes and industries on their current decisions, while a Visiting Scholar at MIT Sloan.

The key to reaching clarity is the ability to focus your physical, mental, and emotional resources, at will, on a certain issue. With this focus, you can identify the right choice faster, more easily, and with greater certainty and internal alignment. It is a practice that can be acquired. This book presents the elements of this practice. The objective of this book is to present techniques that enable you to reach clarity on difficult, strategic decisions with greater effectiveness, thus increasing your decision-making mastery level. This is the book that I wish I could have read at the beginning of my career.

The book defines a Clarity State—a measurable state of mental, physical, and emotional coherence that focuses our inner resources. I found that the combination of the Clarity State with the rigor and discipline of decision-making best practices, utilized by experienced decision makers, has a profound impact on the ability to reach a clear choice in complex situations. This book presents the combination in a practical technique—Clarity State Decision-Making—which can be used by decision makers in small and large organizations alike. Using this process, a stunning 93 percent of CEOs in my test group made clear choices, resolving current decision situations within an hour and a half after focusing on them. Some of these decisions had been pending for weeks or months.

This is truly a new development. Rarely do we know how to summon our internal resources at will, and focus them on an issue to a successful resolution. The approach presented in this book combines traditional, rational ways that we usually use in making decisions, with innovative mind-focusing techniques that enable you to access more brainpower than you normally do.

I invite you to learn and experiment with this technique. Please use this book as a learning tool; choose a current decision that you are working on and take it through the technique. Observe yourself and the level of clarity that you reach with each exercise. Please let me know what you think.

There is no greater reward for an author than to see how people use the book to become better at what they do. If you practice an effective decision-making process, especially by leveraging the Clarity State, you can succeed with consistency. May you have the motivation, creativity, and courage to become a better leader by making more confident, successful, decisions with higher certainty that impact the world in a positive way that is uniquely yours.

Luda Kopeikina
luda@ludakopeikina.com

CHAPTER 1

The Key to Mastering Decisions

Wavering on a decision in critical times can be dangerous! Direct reports sense this state and do not make their decisions in turn, waiting for the decision of the leader. This can lead to a form of paralysis, and the impact on the business can be profound.

Larry Bossidy, Retired Chairman of Honeywell International and Former CEO of Allied Signal[1]

KNOWING HOW TO REACH CLARITY on a decision quickly, especially in critical times, is a differentiating mark of an accomplished leader. It also looks effortless and easy to an observer.

I was privileged to witness master decision makers perform. I sat across from Jack Welch, a former CEO of General Electric, and next to Larry Bossidy, former CEO of Allied Signal, when he was a vice-chairman at General Electric. They made strategic decisions for multimillion- and multi-billion-dollar businesses outwardly effortlessly, based on the information that they just heard and their gut. The impression you get is similar as you watch a great athlete perform.

Michael Jordan's moves on the basketball court, for example, look easy, his shots effortless but stunningly effective.

Behind this mastery is a tremendous effort, a discipline, not visible to the naked eye. In the case of Michael Jordan, it's seven days a week at the gym. In the case of Jack Welch and Larry Bossidy, it is the continuous scrutiny of their decisions and continuous improvement of what they've done in the past—as becomes clear from their books.

In contrast, many of us never question how we make decisions. When we stop to look, we rarely find a method. We usually find a big mess that we inherited from our early years. We discover that sometimes we make random choices, or the decisions are made for us by outside circumstances, and we just comply. Sometimes we make decisions by abdicating our power to a set of rules built into some analytical method or by rebelling against what is expected of us. And sometimes, we decide because we just feel like it.

Key Point
The key to reaching mastery in decision-making is the ability to focus your physical, mental, and emotional resources on an issue like a laser beam. Such focus enables you to reach decision clarity faster and easier.

Focusing on an issue this way or "unleashing a laser beam" is analogous to having an insight or a clarity moment—when a problem that you were thinking about becomes clear in an instant.

This book's approach to decision-making combines traditional, rational ways that you usually use in making decisions with innovative mind-focusing techniques that enable you to access more brainpower than you normally do. The intent is to replicate an effect experienced by a person in a clarity moment.

Mind focusing is supported by the rigor and discipline of decision-making best practices utilized by experienced decision makers, such as decision definition and methods of overcoming decision difficulties. This combination enables deep insights and breakthrough ideas about a decision to surface, paving a faster and easier path to a clear decision.

Experienced executives are better at mind focusing and reaching clarity than novice business managers. Making decisions with clarity faster and easier is a skill, and it can be learned. Reaching mastery in decision-making, however, is the same as reaching mastery in any discipline—it's a product of self-training and discipline that takes effort, understanding, and change.

This is a practical book. The intent is to help you reach a higher level of mastery in your decision-making.

Key Point
The key to mastering decisions is the ability to focus your mind effectively and the process you use to reach clarity.

This book provides you with both—specific methods to focus your mind on a decision and a step-by-step decision-making process to reach clarity. I encourage you to keep a notebook as you read along, do the exercises, think about your current and past decisions, and contemplate your own processes.

Before we get into the details of how to reach a mastery level in decision-making, let's define "clarity in decision-making."

Clarity in Decision Making—Definitions

Clearness is the ornament of profound thought.
Marquis de Vauvenargues[2]

> **Exercise**
> Define clarity in your decision-making. What characteristics of clarity come to mind?

Recollect your own clarity moments.

Where are you usually? What are you doing? It is interesting that in most cases, decision makers say that they are in the shower, driving, or doing something has nothing to do with work.

How are you feeling? When asked, decision makers say "Relaxed," "Enjoying the activity I am involved in," "Not thinking," "Happy," or "Content."

How does the solution arrive? When asked, decision makers say "It just pops into my mind," "I just know," "It's like lightning—things become clear, illuminated," "A lot of thoughts together," or "It's like a laser beam; unimportant things fall away."

How do you feel when the solution arrives? When asked, decision makers say "Excited," "Exhilarated," "Ready to go execute the plan," "Driven," "Determined," or "Very high."

How do you feel about the solution? When asked, decision makers say "I know that this is the right thing to do," "This is it!", or "It's so obvious, why haven't I seen it before? What have I been thinking about?"

One CEO gave me this analogy for how he felt in a clarity moment: "It's as if you are the captain of a ship lost in a fog. You are trying to see the shore and cannot. Then, lightning strikes and illuminates the shore. And then you know where to go, and you are clear on your path and certain that you will get there."

Conventionally, we define "being clear" as reaching a conclusion that is "evident to the mind," unclouded, and free from anything that dims, obscures, or darkens. We also define it as free from doubt or confusion; certain; sure.

I asked business leaders I worked with to define clarity in decision-making as well as to name characteristics that describe a clear decision. One characteristic stood out from these discussions—the inner knowingness, when you know for certain that this is the path you need to take, there are no "ifs" or "buts," you do not doubt, you do not question, you simply know.

> **Definitions**
>
> **Clarity** is a feeling of certainty and of internal alignment with the solution.
>
> **The objective of a decision-making process** is to reach clarity.
>
> **A right decision** is one when the decision maker is emotionally and mentally congruent with it.

Reaching clarity quickly is a differentiating mark of leaders—the trait that is visible to observers. For example, biographers of President Reagan stress again and again that he was always certain about his choices and was able to quickly reach clarity on decisions.

> **Exercise**
>
> Recollect a decision you made with certainty and internal align-
> ment. How did it feel? Now recollect a decision you made without
> certainty. How did it feel? What was the difference between the
> two? Be specific.

Characteristics of a Clear Decision

The most common sort of lie is the one uttered to one's self.
Friedrich Nietzsche[3]

The trick, of course, is to know when you have reached certainty on
your decision and to differentiate such situations from the times when
you are fooling yourself. In our discussions about clarity in decision-
making, many business executives stressed the following three characteristics of reaching a clear decision.

Positive Charge

Reaching clarity in a decision is a tremendously positive experience. A
decision maker gets charged with the excitement, the energy, and the
power of the vision behind the decision and the eventual business ac-
complishment that this choice will lead to.

Obviously, when a decision necessitates an action that would be
detrimental to a party or parties involved, such as a layoff, you do not
feel happy, but rather determined, confident in the need to take the action and in the ability to get it accomplished successfully. It is still a
positive emotion that allows you to move forward with gusto, power,
and confidence.

In other words, if you are making a major strategic decision and
feel "blah" about it, try again, because you have not found the right
solution.

Commitment to a Vision

After discussion, my immediate reports always knew whether or not I made the decision. And usually, when I did, they lined up and focused on execution.

Larry Bossidy, Retired Chairman of Honeywell International and Former CEO of Allied Signal[4]

Arriving at a clear decision after a potentially long and difficult process of looking for the right solution unleashes not only a feeling of excitement or determination in a decision maker, but also a feeling of commitment to a particular vision. This internal alignment and commitment cannot be faked and are visible to subordinates and other parties involved in the execution of a decision.

Minimal Post-Decision Doubts

One major characteristic of a decision reached with clarity is that post-decision doubts are minimized. The number of post-decision doubts during the solution implementation can serve as a verification of whether you reached the right decision.

Go back to your recollection of a decision you made through a clarity moment. How did you feel after the decision was made and you were in the process of executing it? Did you have many doubts? When asked, decision makers say "No doubts whatsoever!" or "We might have changed the path slightly because new information arrived, but no doubts, no..."

Now recollect a difficult decision you made without a feeling of certainty that it was right for you and the business. You might have been pressed for time, looked at all the options, and just picked the one that was the best in your judgment. Did you come back to it later with questions like "Should we have looked at it from another angle?" or "Have we miscalculated? Should we have gone with another option?"? It is common to feel doubtful if the decision was not reached with clarity.

Making *any* decision may increase your confidence in that decision due to a common cognitive phenomenon that researchers call a "post-decision dissonance reduction[5]." In most decisions, a selected alternative has some negative features, and the rejected alternatives have some positive features. This situation creates an inconsistency or dissonance in the mind of the decision maker and a desire to create additional cognitive support for the chosen alternative after the decision is made. This phenomenon is also called "bolstering of the chosen alternative[6,7]."

Bolstering is not necessary when you reach a clear decision in the definition provided earlier in this chapter—when you are internally aligned with the solution emotionally and mentally. No question mark is left in your mind when the decision is made—the choice is certain and clear. When you have to lean on bolstering, it means that you have not reached the certainty level needed for a clear decision.

If you must continually convince yourself that your decision was right after you have made it, you are on the wrong path!

The Value of Decision Clarity

Through my executive experience, I have come to appreciate the value of clarity in decision-making. Not only does a clear decision save time, eliminate unnecessary actions, and release energy into acting, but it also enables a leader to project commitment to a vision and allows the whole team to focus on execution, which is paramount to a successful implementation.

Key Point
You cannot lead without reaching clarity first!

Clarity Enables the Leader to Project Commitment to a Chosen Path and Eliminates Confusion

> *When you know it's right, you'll make it right.*
> *Keith Collins, CEO of PhyTrust, Inc.[8]*

Most interviewed business leaders talked about the importance of getting to clarity or inner certainty about a decision as quickly as possible. It is critically important for the management team to see the leader's commitment to the chosen path. This commitment can come only when the leader unequivocally reaches a clear decision that is accompanied with an internal commitment to reaching a goal through a chosen path.

As I mentioned before, this inner certainty cannot be faked and is visible to the other people involved. What's happening on the inside shows on the outside. Seeing this commitment, the team usually puts extra effort into reaching the objective better and faster.

Exercise

Think of an objective (political, business, or personal) that you do not morally support or do not believe is achievable. Imagine that you need to lead a team to implement it. How would you do it? What would you need to do in order to be successful? Rate your probability of success.

Clarity Saves Time and Eliminates Unnecessary Actions

Reaching the right decision quickly can save weeks or months of frustrating indecision and uncertainty. The time spent on achieving clarity pays back in solutions that reach your objective through the fastest route, eliminating unnecessary diversions. In fact, you might be surprised when you find yourself taking actions that are entirely different from what you would have done without reaching clarity first. You eliminate perhaps 80 percent or more of the unnecessary actions you would have taken.

The following case demonstrates how one half hour spent in considering a decision and reaching clarity can eliminate unnecessary actions and keep you from spending months on a slower path.

EXAMPLE 1-1: DOUG—SHOW SYNDICATION DECISION

Doug is the CEO of a marketing company. He is also a well-known persona on radio and TV. He has been running a radio show for the last four years and has developed a brand in a particular market. However, financially, the show has not performed to his expectations. It has been around break-even from its inception, not making much money. Currently, Doug sees an opportunity to syndicate the show across the country with a potential to make a return on the time and effort that have been invested in the show.

In order for the show to become a major force in the U.S. market, however, Doug has to invest his personal time and other resources to develop the show further—a major concern for him, given his current efforts.

Disregarding this concern, he pushes ahead with his normal attitude: "We'll get it done somehow." His calendar is busy with meetings related to the show expansion and potential syndication.

Doug decides to consider this situation using the clarity state decision-making process described later in the book. During the exercise, Doug realizes that there is no pressing need to expand the show now; nothing dramatic will change if he does not act on it at this time. Rather, he can focus on the current critical business efforts and get them to a successful resolution faster, and only then take on the show syndication. "Besides," he decides, "if we wait with the syndication, the opportunity to leverage the radio show across various other efforts will be much higher and might produce a much bigger impact."

Doug is a very successful, active person who, similar to many of us, likes to act on an opportunity that presents itself and becomes frustrated when he cannot do so because of time commitment to other efforts.

Spending just half an hour in contemplation of the situation, he reaches a clear decision to postpone the show syndication for six months. This decision clarity is beneficial to him in three ways: a) it enables him to cross off several time-intensive action items from his to-do list, thus freeing his time; b) it enables him to focus on other efforts; and c) it allows other marketing efforts within the company to mature to a point where a syndicated radio show can leverage them and, as a result, produce a much bigger impact on Doug's overall business. Was it worth reaching this clarity?

Clarity Releases Energy into Acting

Achieving clarity in a decision focuses your energy as well as the energy of your team on moving forward in executing the decision and achieving results rather than in being in a "deciding mode"—a state that many decision makers find frustrating and energy-draining. Another problem with the state of indecision that can be avoided when

clarity is reached is wasting the company's resources by allowing different teams to pursue different courses of action until a clear decision is
made and communicated.

Exercise

Recollect your past three major decisions that you had to "wrestle"
with. How long were you in the "deciding mode"? Why?

Clarity Allows Flexibility in Tactics and Implementation

When interviewed, decision makers stressed that reaching clarity usually means alignment with the *vision* behind the decision and not with
the specifics of the implementation plan. Often, additional information
becomes available after the decision is made that might require a
change in the implementation tactics. The alignment with the broad
objective rather than implementation details makes it easier to alter the
tactics if necessary—provided, of course, that the overall implementation plan still leads to the target. As a result, a clear decision enables
much more flexibility in the implementation, as opposed to cases when
a decision maker just settles on a course of action without clarity.

Right Decision and Decision Quality

*Everything we do has a result. But that which is right and prudent does
not always lead to good, nor the contrary to what is bad.*

Goethe[9]

Earlier in this chapter, I defined a decision as clear or right when it is
aligned with the decision maker at the time of the decision. Notice that
*arriving at a right decision in this definition does not guarantee good
consequences of a post-decision state of affairs.*

Exercise

How do you judge your and other people's decisions?

If you are a conventionalist, you judge a decision by its consequences. Because you cannot fully foresee the consequences at the moment of making the decision, you will be under the spell of fear of not making the right choice. If you are a revolutionary leader, like Walt Disney, you judge your decision by the degree of its alignment with your vision.

As leaders, we are paid to select strategies that "increase value to shareholders," "increase sales," and "improve effectiveness"—strategies that will deliver the best consequences to the business. All our decisions are made with these major objectives in mind. Given the higher-than-average competitiveness of this group, we are always on the lookout for strategies that will place our businesses ahead of competition and enable them to reach the status of "industry leader."

Therefore, as leaders, when we make a decision, we select a solution that will lead to the best consequences in our judgment. We also *take responsibility* for the consequences, independent of whether they turn out to be good or bad. Only those who are prepared to bear the consequences of a decision have the right to make it.

Experts in decision-making and negotiation techniques John Hammond, Ralph Keeney, and Howard Raiffa agree: "Although many people judge the quality of their own and others' decisions by the quality of the consequences—by how things turn out—this is an erroneous view[10]."

Why?

Most strategic decisions involve uncertainty. When uncertainty is involved, a decision maker must foresee how things will evolve in the future when a proposed action is taken. Because you cannot predict the future, there can be no guarantees of how a decision will turn out—whether it will have good or bad consequences. The market, along with other forces, can interfere and change the environment. As a result, a good decision can turn out badly, and a bad decision can turn out well.

Consider the following example, in which a decision that was not thoroughly evaluated turns out well.

EXAMPLE 1-2: ELLEN—A POOR DECISION TURNS OUT WELL

Ellen is the CEO of a public software company. She took the role two years ago with an objective to find and execute strategies to dramatically grow the company. The strategy that the company embarked on under her leadership is a combination of organic growth in certain market segments where the company's products are highly differentiated and acquisitions in others.

Her team looks for a good acquisition for 12 months. After the initial discussions with three selected targets, only one company remains under consideration. The due diligence highlights several issues, but the team recommends going ahead and completing the transaction. Ellen agrees.

Six months after the acquisition, concerns that were highlighted during the due diligence (related to product integration) have been assessed to be more serious than was initially estimated. A much larger investment than initially estimated is now required in order to bring acquired products in line with the other products in the company's portfolio. Privately, Ellen starts thinking that this acquisition has been a mistake.

The acquisition adds five software products to the company's portfolio. Suddenly, the demand for one of them, a simple web application, starts to grow. In the case of this application, there are no issues related to integration with other products. The higher sales of this new application "pull through" the company's other products. As a result, Ellen's company is about to report higher-than-projected quarterly revenue numbers.

Did Ellen make a good decision to go through with the acquisition? She admits that the answer is no. However, if you did not know the details of the story, your outside assessment would have been that this acquisition was a success. But the success was unexpected and unforeseen.

Next, let's consider an example when a perfectly good undertaking goes badly.

EXAMPLE 1-3: MARK—A GOOD DECISION TURNS OUT BADLY

Mark is the CEO of a company. The company's security product is based on a mathematical cryptography algorithm developed by four expert mathematicians who are professors at different universities. Mark was brought in by these founders to run the company. Mark is successful in raising $40 million and signing contracts with a number of Fortune 50 customers. The company is doing well, expanding and on the path to go public.

Six years into the company's life, one of the customers discovers a "bug" in the product, which, after investigation, turns out to be a flaw in the main algorithm on which the product is based. Several months of intensive work looking for a fix turn out no promising results. The company's main operations are now being closed. Only a small consulting unit will remain in business. Most of the money will be returned to investors.

Did the founders make a good decision to open a company based on their research? The answer is a resounding yes. Were they justified in taking money from investors and signing contracts with customers? This answer is also yes.

It is common in the security software industry, however, to find problems with an algorithm during the first 10 years after the algorithm starts being used. Were the founders aware of this risk? Yes. Were they willing to take this risk? Yes. Unfortunately, in their case, this risk materialized. As a result, the consequences to those involved, such as founders, employees, investors, and customers, were not good.

Exercise

How would you evaluate the quality of your or your subordinate's major decision? What parameters would you use?

Experts advise that "decisions under uncertainty should be judged by the quality of decision-making, not by the quality of the consequences[10]."

There are two major sets of decision quality parameters. One set is related to the quality of the decision-making *process* (such as its organization and rigor), and another set is related to the quality of the decision-making *content* (such as the depth and breadth of considered decision parameters and specific information related to the decision)[11].

Inherent in the decision-making process presented in this book are standard parameters of decision quality included in these sets. For example, a good decision-making process requires that a business objective and an outstanding business need be addressed. It requires selecting an option that is better than others in satisfying the main objective and is projected to bring the best outcome to the business.

My definition adds a third evaluation factor—the level of internal alignment with the decision that brings extra clarity to the decision maker and, with it, the benefits I discussed before—commitment, flexibility, and a positive drive to execute the decision.

Here are the decision quality evaluation factors:

- Quality of the decision-making process
- Quality of the decision-making content
- Quality of internal alignment with your vision

We should judge a decision by the quality of the decision-making process, the quality of the data utilized in making the decision, and the degree of internal alignment with the decision maker.

Assignment

I encourage you to select a current situation that you need to resolve that you can use throughout the book as a sample decision.

Select a decision that is nontrivial, one you have been thinking about. It can be a personal decision or a business decision. Make sure that it is an important decision that you do not want to make lightly. You might or might not be ready to decide how to resolve the situation. Write down the decision question in your notebook. You will be working with this decision in each chapter of the book.

CHAPTER 2

The Clarity State—Mental Focus Redefined

The strong man is the one who is able to intercept at will the communication between the senses and the mind.

Napoleon Bonaparte[1]

IN A CLARITY MOMENT, INSIGHTS ARE TRIGGERED, things fall into place, and a solution becomes obvious and clear. Unfortunately, clarity moments happen *to us*; we cannot *make* them happen. If you are wrestling with a tough situation, though you may try to reach clarity by force, it will most likely elude you. There has not been, until this book, a defined method or technique to gain clarity at will.

Key Point

Clarity State is intended to replicate a state of being in the clarity moment. This state is instrumental to making tough choices faster, more easily, and with better internal alignment.

If clarity moments come for free—that is, they just happen to us—obtaining clarity at will requires mental effort—using your mind in a certain way.

Clarity comes from a state of mental concentration, of focusing thoughts and paying attention. Clarity is reached by training the mind to be precise and accurate in its definitions, assumptions, and evaluations.

Sounds easy, doesn't it? You sit down, focus on the problem, and achieve clarity. But this doesn't work in most cases, does it? Why not?

It is because in most cases we are not in the right state of mind—we are stressed, anxious, or worried about something, and our bodies cannot relax without first making an effort to overcome these feelings of anxiety and worry. Or, it is because in many cases our bodies are tense, and as a result, our minds cannot get calm and concentrated under these conditions either.

In other words, the state for obtaining clarity has a number of prerequisites, the first one being physical relaxation, and the second being emotional balance. It is similar to the state that athletes train to achieve. Over the last 20 years, athletes have learned that physical, emotional, and mental coherence is required for peak performance.

The definition of the Clarity State is based on lessons learned from peak performance training in sports and recent neuroscience research.

Definition

Clarity State is the state of being

- Physically relaxed
- Emotionally positive, happy, released from fear and anxiety
- Charged with power, success, self-confidence, and energy
- Totally in the present
- Mentally focused on the task at hand

Figure 2-1 presents this definition in graphical terms and further identifies parameters of the Clarity State.

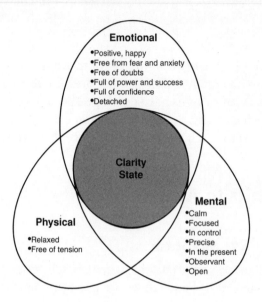

Emotional
- Positive, happy
- Free from fear and anxiety
- Free of doubts
- Full of power and success
- Full of confidence
- Detached

Clarity State

Mental
- Calm
- Focused
- In control
- Precise
- In the present
- Observant
- Open

Physical
- Relaxed
- Free of tension

FIGURE 2-1
Clarity State

In this state, athletes report a sense of being in control, but not the type of control that requires exertion of effort—rather, a definite sense of being able to make the right moves with the intended results. They also report a sense of inner calm and of being acutely aware of their bodies and their environment, with an ability to anticipate correctly other people's moves.

Most of us know this state very well. Executives told me stories about making an important, usually strategic, business decision while being on vacation. Usually, it was a decision that lingered for months before they went on vacation. They described their state of mind at the moment of making the decision in almost exactly the same words that I am using in the definition of the Clarity State—being relaxed, positive, happy, and feeling successful. In fact, several of them mentioned that the whole intent of going on vacation at that time was to reach this state, hoping that the outstanding decision would become clearer.

> **Exercise**
> Review your last week, and identify the number of times you were
> in this state during business hours. How about last month?

If you did not find many occurrences of this state in your schedule,
do not despair—you are not alone. Under pressure to perform in stress-
ful circumstances, most of us have developed behaviors that are death
habits to achieving clarity. Seekers of decision clarity, true business
leaders who want to reach clarity quickly, have to avoid the following.

Death Habits to Achieving Clarity

Death Habit #1: Multitask

In the current business environment, where there is more work in each
job position than can be handled, we are taught to multitask. Conventional wisdom says "Never lose a moment—if you are talking on the
phone, scan your e-mails at the same time." The result is that we never
have time to focus!

This habit is in sharp contrast to the behavior that peak performers
in sports train to achieve. Successful athletes know that when every
physical and mental resource is focused, your power to perform multi-
plies tremendously.

Key Point
In order to outperform others, you have to learn to
focus your resources!

Public awareness of the power of mental training started at the
1976 Olympics, when Russia won more gold medals than any other
country. The East German team placed second, its women swimmers
taking 11 of the 13 medals. The United States placed third.

These results were so extraordinary that, initially, the use of steroids
was widely suspected. Slowly, the truth began to trickle through the
Iron Curtain—Soviet athletes were utilizing mental training. Results

from studies started to become available in the late '70s. Charles Garfield, a world-renowned expert on mental athlete training, recounts one study[2] in which four carefully matched groups of athletes trained for several weeks, with the following regiments:

- Group I—100% physical training
- Group II—75% physical training and 25% mental training
- Group III—50% physical training and 50% mental training
- Group IV—25% physical training and 75% mental training

Group IV had shown significantly greater improvement than Group III, with Groups II and I following, in that order. These studies showed unequivocally that mental training is paramount for peak performance.

This mental training includes developing the ability to quickly relax one's body. It also includes developing the ability to quickly shift negative emotions into positive ones and to be in a positive emotional state. And, most importantly, it includes developing the ability to maintain this state of physical relaxation, emotional control, and mental focus that athletes call "athletic poise." This is a state of psychological readiness and mental preparedness that is known to be a prerequisite for peak performance.

Training programs for peak performance, such as the one developed by Garfield based on his work with Soviet trainers and athletes around the world, are now the norm in the training regimen of serious athletes.

The habit of multitasking splinters our resources and prevents us from developing and executing at peak performance levels.

Death Habit #2: Be Competitive

Do not misunderstand me. Competing with yourself is a great habit— pushing yourself to excel at your job, learn new skills faster, develop new competencies, or whatever challenges you want to conquer is a habit worth nurturing. Few people during their lifetime exhaust the resources hidden within them. There are deep wells of strength in each of us that are never used. Learning to tap into this inner power is a worthy pursuit.

But the way people understand the conventional wisdom is "Be competitive with others." In such an interpretation, the measures of progress become outside metrics—assessment of your performance by others, comparing your status with the status of your coworkers, and so on. The problem is that these outside measures are usually outside of your control. Striving to measure your progress by outside metrics undoubtedly creates stress and negative emotions, such as anxiety and worry. The more you strive to deliver results according to outside metrics, the more stress and pain you create in your life.

Recent research in the field of neuroscience tells us that under the spell of stress and negative emotions, the human brain gets into a state of "cortical inhibition"—a desynchronization or reduction of cortical activity during which several areas of the brain are effectively shut down[3]. Neuroscientists warn, "This condition can manifest in less efficient decision-making capabilities, leading to poor or shortsighted decisions, ineffective or impulsive communication, and reduced physical coordination[4]."

The habit of being competitive with others leads us to accumulate stress in our lives and perform at less than optimal capacity.

Death Habit #3: Work All the Time and Do More

We are becoming a nation of workaholics. With the advances of cell phones and the Internet, our work is with us all the time—at the dinner table, at the outing with the kids on the beach, and so on. If we let it, our workload can consume us, proliferate stress, and, as a result, lead to continuous operation at a lower brain capacity. You need to save some mental, physical, and emotional resources to regenerate, think, and strategize for the future.

Neuroscience researchers have shown that when a certain level of physical and emotional coherence is reached, the areas of the brain that are usually shut down under stress become available to us[3]. This extra "mental power" can be harnessed at will and utilized to solve problems and address difficult situations[5].

Physiologically, the state of coherence is a phenomenon whereby systems exhibiting periodic behavior synchronize and oscillate at the same frequency and phase. Neuroscientists explain, "This state represents a highly efficient mode of bodily function and is associated with heightened clarity, buoyancy, and inner peace[3]."

Researchers have also proven that in this state of "entrainment" or "coherence," cognitive ability improves[6].

Our workaholic tendency prevents us from taking time to contemplate, focus our minds on critical issues, and utilize our full brain capacity and cognitive ability for developing creative solutions.

Breaking Death Habits

He who conquers others is strong; he who conquers himself is mighty.

Lao Tse[7]

Inherent in the definition of the Clarity State are the behaviors required for breaking the death habits to reaching clarity. The definition shares similarities with the state of athletic poise. Clarity State *is* the state of coherence that is required for improved cognitive activity.

Key Point
Clarity State, a state of physical, emotional, and mental coherence, is known to be a precursor of peak performance in athletic competitions. It is also known to enable the clearing of blockages in our physical system, allowing us to utilize more of our brain capacity and improve cognitive function.

This is a powerful state. It can be reached quickly (in 5 to 10 minutes) and at will (whenever you need it). Just being in this state three times a day for a couple minutes has been proven to be a powerful de-stressor and effectiveness booster.

A moment's insight is sometimes worth a life's experience.

Oliver Wendell Holmes, Sr.[8]

In decision-making, this state has a profound impact on a person's ability to reach a clear choice. When business leaders used this state for decision-making in my study, they usually experienced insights about their current situations. The decision makers commonly shifted a perspective or found a critical parameter that immediately pointed to the right solution.

Let me give you an example.

EXAMPLE 2-1: KEN—RESTRUCTURING A PORTFOLIO

Ken is a CEO of an investment-banking firm. He is contemplating a decision about how to restructure a specific portfolio, taking into account the current changes in the economy and the interest rates.

He is fascinated by the fact that in the past, he made similar decisions without any difficulty. He was able to think about various options and move forward in a matter of days. This time, for some reason, he could not decide what to do.

Here is Ken's feedback after he went through the exercise: "Quite suddenly I realized that the crux of the issue was not how to structure the portfolio but my fear of making a mistake. The technical way to restructure it is obvious. However, any change in this portfolio carries a significant degree of risk. I am planning semi-retirement in a couple of years. What if I'm not there to fix it if I make a mistake in this restructuring?"

What happened?

Ken had a personal objective (to retire with all his affairs in order) that he was not consciously aware of as being part of this decision. When he realized the crux of the issue that was preventing him from making a decision, the decision itself became obvious and clear.

Learning to reach and then utilize the Clarity State—for decisions in difficult business and personal situations—can unleash the power of insight that lies inside every one of us and thus can sharpen our decision-making and leadership abilities.

CHAPTER 3

Five Hurdles to Clarity

Nothing is more difficult, and therefore more precious, than to be able to decide.

Napoleon Bonaparte[1]

Business managers make many decisions. Among them are many simple decisions that they make easily during the day. There are also more complex decisions where many parameters need to be considered, many of them riddled with assumptions and uncertainty. Usually these decisions are strategic, such as selecting a market strategy, choosing an acquisition target, or opting for an integration strategy for two companies. These decisions require analysis of financial data, evaluation of marketing assumptions, assessment of team capabilities, and much more.

Usually, these decisions are not only complex but also difficult because they often carry an enormous degree of risk for a decision maker, both business and personal, and often, they cannot be easily reversed. Sometimes the decision is made even more difficult when the decision maker's team is not in agreement on the strategy, and it's even more difficult when the rational mind says one thing but your gut another.

In this spectrum of decisions, from simple to difficult, I focus on the ones that require a "Let's think about it" response from a decision maker, the ones from the middle of the spectrum to the most difficult. I am especially interested in decisions that *experienced* decision makers consider *most difficult,* the ones where, in the process of trying to arrive at a solution, a person has exhausted common methods of resolving decision difficulties and yet has not reached a clear solution. Methods used might have included talking to team members and trusted advisors, collecting additional information, using analytical tools, and considering pros and cons of each alternative.

> ### Exercise
> Recollect three difficult decisions you had to make over the last several years. Why were they difficult for you? Write down these three decisions. Also note why you considered them difficult.

By focusing on the most difficult decisions of experienced decision makers I interviewed, I wanted to *understand how they come to regard some decisions as difficult and why.* My aim is practical in nature. Understanding difficulties can be instructive in learning to overcome them. Because we often get "stuck" in making decisions, I wanted to know why this is the case and how we can get "unstuck."

The process of making difficult decisions requires from a leader focused mental energy, a "vision" power, and an ability to transcend the present and at the same time be realistic about the abilities of the leader and his or her company. Experienced decision makers have developed their own unique methods of overcoming decision difficulties as well as their own unique ways of making difficult decisions. I compiled these precious ideas and incorporated them into the decision-making technique described in this book.

In discussing past business decisions, I not only asked about the perceived decision difficulty at the time of the decision but also probed for root causes behind this perceived difficulty.

In the interviews, leaders commonly cited difficulties that were vague, such as "It just didn't feel right," "All solutions had risk involved, and we were trying to figure out the consequences of all options; it was tough, and I felt anxious," or "It just wasn't clear; all options under consideration somehow did not address our main need." I had to dig deeper by asking "why" a number of times to actually get at the reasons behind the difficulties.

It was also common for a decision to have a number of difficulties associated with it, such as "I was very emotionally vested in the situation and could not sleep nights. We were under enormous time pressure—we needed to do something urgently! We also had to invest money that we did not have at the time—very risky... and the whole thing was not clear at all." In those cases, I had to ask a lot of questions before we could identify the main reason why the decision seemed difficult.

I grouped root causes behind decision difficulties into five major categories:

- Lack of a clear objective
- Lack of clear constraints
- Difficulty in dealing with emotions (such as fear, guilt, and regret, or emotions resulting from a disagreement)
- Lack of a clear perspective (frame)
- Difficulty in selecting from among options

Exercise

As you go through the following examples, work with the three decisions you recollected in the previous exercise. For each decision, identify a root cause behind the difficulty of your decision.

The point of this exercise is for you to identify a specific type of difficulty that is most common in your decision-making. You might want to reflect on more than three tough decisions of the past in order to identify this commonality.

Let me demonstrate the categories through examples. In each example, I highlight the perceived difficulty or difficulties that the interviewee stated initially during the interview.

Lack of a Clear Objective

An ignorance of means may minister

To greatness, but an ignorance of aims

Makes it impossible to be great at all.

Elizabeth Barrett Browning[2]

In many cases, the situation forces the decision maker to evaluate options—"Should I do this or that?"—without consciously recognizing it. The following example demonstrates this phenomenon.

EXAMPLE 3-1: JOHN—ACCEPTING A CEO POSITION

John's company (TRL) was acquired by a public company (MPC) a little over a year ago. After the acquisition, John became a Vice President of Development at MPC. He had successfully leveraged the international development capability brought to MPC by the TRL acquisition and managed to bring MPC to profitability and to maintain it over the last four quarters—a major achievement.

However, he is starting to see serious danger signs in the company's ability to grow. He now believes that he and his TRL partner seriously overestimated MPC's distribution capabilities at the time of the acquisition. These capabilities are limited to a contract with one major distributor. The market growth for MPC's products is slowing, and the lack of other distribution channels is about to put MPC into a major financial crisis.

A month ago, John finally realized that MPC is "heading into a wall" and started thinking about the company's options. In his discussion of the situation with board members, an organizational restructuring was suggested in which the current CEO (Todd) leaves the company and John becomes the new CEO. Now John is faced with a decision—to take the role or not. He does not want to be the CEO, but he does not see any other options. He decides to take the CEO role. He is not happy with the decision, and he feels a lot of uncertainty and anxiety.

John stated his difficulty in making this decision as follows: "It was difficult because I was about to lose all the work we put into building our company over these years. Naturally, I was emotional and wanted to set it right immediately. It was not clear how to proceed in order to fix the situation."

What is John's objective in making this decision? His objectives could have been as follows:

1. Maximize financial benefit from his overall investment, first in TRL, and then in MPC.
2. Save the company by embarking on a different strategy.
3. Do something, because the situation is getting worse.

The problem was that John never asked himself this question. If he had the first objective, the ousting of Todd was not the solution—selling the company was. With his relationships in the industry, Todd would have been the most instrumental agent for such a move. In retrospect, John believes that selling the company would have been the right option that would have satisfied all parties concerned.

John's objective was not the second one, either. It is true that at the time of the decision, he was thinking about saving the company. However, he readily admits that he did not have a clear strategy for how to save it. The best way to describe his objective at this time is "Something needs to be done."

Essentially, the situation itself—a deteriorating financial position, for which current management was to blame, and the board's conviction that because John had made the company profitable, he could also reshape it for the future—imposed solution options by forcing John to decide quickly and consider only obvious options that were available to him. If he had taken the time to define his objective, his decision would have been different. He would have talked to Todd and convinced him that the company needed to be sold while it had strong profitability and strong intellectual capital. Now, in retrospect, he believes that this is exactly what he should have done.

Over the first year after becoming a CEO, John experimented with different growth options. However, the revenue kept sliding, slowly but surely. He had to execute several layoffs and finally sold the company for much less than the value at the time of his initial decision to take the CEO role. He now believes that he made a "wrong" decision by taking the company's helm.

John is not alone. The tendency to "plunge in" to the solution before defining the decision and its objective is one of the main traps in decision-making[3]. Most people spend too little time and effort on the task of specifying objectives. Granted, it is not an easy task—identifying objectives is an art[4].

In my work with business executives on their current decisions, I selected several easy ways to quickly identify the main decision objective. I have also seen that Clarity State has a major impact on clarifying the objective in the mind of a decision maker. I will discuss both topics later in the book.

Exercise

Rate the clarity of your objective in the three past decisions that you selected in the first exercise on a scale of 1 to 5, with 1 being lowest and 5 being highest. Write down your average score. Determine whether you consider "defining decision objectives" as an area for improvement in your decision-making.

Lack of Clear Constraints

Nothing, unless it is difficult, is worthwhile.

Ovid[5]

Clarity of an objective is very important, but unless all major parameters of the decision are added to the objective, the decision is not well defined. When this is the case, it's likely that the solution will not be clear. Decision makers describe the difficulty of such situations as follows: "Something was bothering me. I felt that I was missing something important, but I wasn't sure what it was."

Constraint is a condition that a decision maker imposes on a solution. Any parameter that is worth considering, any discomfort area related to the decision, and any difficulty can be defined as a constraint. Because decisions usually have a number of objectives, secondary objectives can be defined as constraints as well. The problem is that in real life, decision makers rarely clearly identify major parameters involved in a decision.

Unfortunately, when you have a missing constraint, several things can go wrong with the decision: some options may look possible when in reality they are not, certain options may not be considered at all, and the decision may not become clear overall for a longer period of time.

There is also a problem of perceived constraints—parameters that are addressable in ways unrelated to the decision. Accepting such constraints into the decision definition carries the danger of unnecessarily limiting the scope of potential solutions.

I found from interviews that a number of areas related to decision-making are commonly overlooked. The following list is just a sample of such areas:

- **Conflict with corporate culture**—A decision maker "sells" himself or herself on a course of action that is in conflict with how the company operates in accordance with its unwritten rules.

- **Availability of people critical to the venture**—A manager launches a new initiative, assuming incorrectly that certain people are available for this effort.

- **Realism of the proposed solution**—The organization's ability to execute the solution.

- **Internal conflict**—Rational reasoning says one thing, but the decision maker believes it is wrong somehow.

- **Biased assumptions**—People's reactions, market assumptions, cash requirement projections, and other parameters of the decision may be based on old patterns that have changed or are changing.

- **Personal issues**—A decision maker might have a personal objective that is not consciously taken into account and that might be in conflict with the proposed business strategy.

I discuss some of these areas in more detail in Chapter 7, "Escaping Handcuffs—How to Achieve Clarity of Constraints."

The following example demonstrates how reaching clarity on one such critical parameter helped a CEO take a better course of action.

EXAMPLE 3-2: ALAN—EVALUATING AN ACQUISITION

Alan is the CEO of a software company. The company embarked on an acquisition strategy in order to add applications to its software product suite. The company is evaluating one such acquisition. Intellectually, the acquisition makes a lot of sense to Alan. In his gut, however, it doesn't feel right; something is missing.

In describing how he felt at that time, he compares himself to a groom right before the marriage ceremony who doubts his decision to marry. He felt that he was being forced into a hurried decision about this acquisition—as if he were in the church for a rushed marriage that did not feel quite right.

Flying back from a visit to the company being acquired, he realizes that the person he put in charge of the due diligence process and whom he was planning to put in charge of the acquired company would not be able to handle the job. It felt like a "click"—he instantly realized that this was the issue that was bothering him.

What was Alan's objective? It's clear: "Grow the business through finding and acquiring a good company that has products with certain functionality." Even though Alan's initial description of the decision's difficulty was that it just did not feel right, the actual difficulty was the concern that his senior management team was not ready to integrate this acquisition successfully. In fact, he did not have a person to run the acquired company. The clarity of this constraint enabled Alan to move forward with the acquisition but with a management arrangement different from what he previously envisioned.

Alan is not alone. In fact, in at least a quarter of business decision cases, decision makers found new constraints while contemplating their current decisions in the Clarity State. This highlights the problem—some parameters of a decision are elusive. Personal interests, for example, are often not taken into account. Concerns related to a decision are usually present, but decision makers rarely take time to verbalize them.

I discovered that being in the Clarity State helps in identifying and clarifying such elusive parameters, as you will explore later in the book. When such parameters are clearly identified, more options might become available, certain options may become feasible when they were not before, or the whole decision may become clear.

> ### Exercise
>
> Recollect a past decision experience when things didn't feel quite right. Looking back at that situation, do you see certain dimensions of the situation that were missing from your consideration at the time of the decision?
>
> Recollect an experience when you were surprised by the turn of events after you made the decision. What factor could you have taken into account in your decision in order to be better prepared—the one you knew but missed?
>
> How often do these types of situations happen in your decision-making? Write down your decision. Note whether "constraints clarification" is an area for improvement for you.

Difficulty in Dealing with Emotions

Fire is the test of gold; adversity, of strong men.

Seneca[6]

It was rare to discuss a difficult decision during an interview in which a decision maker was not involved emotionally. I found that a range of negative emotions were involved: fear, guilt, frustration, and regret. There were several cases where an already complex decision was complicated by a disagreement within a management team, with the board, or with investors.

In many cases, the decision had serious *personal* implications. Decision makers believed, some consciously and at the time of the decision, others subconsciously and in retrospect, that if a wrong decision were made, it would adversely affect their career. Such realization added more stress and anxiety to the decision-making process.

The following is just one demonstration of how emotionally difficult some decisions can get.

EXAMPLE 3-3: GEORGE—ADJUSTING A COMPANY'S FINANCIAL STRUCTURE

George is the CEO of a profitable company with $425M in revenue. The company is highly leveraged; the financial structure looks like this:

- Bank debt of $550M (33 banks participating with a lead bank)
- Public bonds of $150M
- Eighty percent of the equity is owned by equity firms, most of them on the company's board
- Management owns the remainder of the equity; George has a portion of this 20 percent

The company started to feel refinancing pressure when the market slowed down. Operationally, the company was working well; it was the fastest growing company in the industry and one of the largest. George realized that on top of his operational responsibilities, he had to reconcile the investor constituencies that were pulling in different directions: banks, equity firms, and bondholders. Obviously, because he had equity in the company, his natural alignment would have been with the company's equity holders. However, he was trying to do what was right for the company. Unfortunately, the equity holders did not want to put together a permanent financing solution and were proposing to just extend the current agreements for a year.

George went along with this proposal and spent six months negotiating an amendment to the current financing structure, which cost the company $9 million. Six months later, it became clear that the second amendment was required. The company needed cash and had to cut back staff, even though operationally there was no such need. The crux of the difficulty was that George wanted to put together a more permanent financing structure that would have lasted three to five years. Such a solution would have necessitated equity holders to give in on their secured-by-the-contract financial position, the approach they resisted.

George decided to go to the outside investment banker for advice and other options. The word got out to the lead equity holder who had hired George into the CEO role. George was told that he was not "playing straight" and was not cooperating. In his words, "This started the strained relationship that never recovered."

George decided to leave the company at the end of 2002. He feels totally "right" about his decision, because he followed his sense of integrity, which rebelled against doing what was not right for the company. However, the departure left him with a feeling of failure.

Talking about his final decision to leave the company, George assessed the difficulty in the following way: "I felt that I was asked to carry out a course of action that I did not feel was right. I was making a tremendous positive impact on the company on the operational side, but this internal conflict and the conflict with investment bankers made it difficult for me to run the company productively."

You can imagine a CEO who would have gone through the trials and tribulations of George's experience without getting emotionally involved. But it is hard to stay emotionally uninvolved when one's job satisfaction, success, and personal compensation are at stake. Having a disagreement with a major stakeholder in the company also adds a load of emotional burden to the decision maker.

The subject of dealing with emotions in decision-making is mired in a number of cultural beliefs. I review the recent science findings vis-à-vis these beliefs and discuss a number of techniques that decision makers found instrumental in dealing with emotions utilizing the Clarity State in Chapter 8, "Balancing Mind and Body—How to Learn from Your Emotional Cues." Chapter 9, "Pick a Fight!—How to Get the Most Out of Clashing Opinions," is devoted to dealing with disagreements and leveraging them as constructive tools to reach clarity.

Exercise

Recollect a past decision experience that was extremely emotional for you. Looking back at that situation, was it the decision itself or the communication of the decision that caused an emotional response? How effective were you in handling the situation? Rate your effectiveness. Write down this decision, and note whether dealing with emotions is one of the areas for improvement in your decision-making.

Lack of a Clear Perspective (Frame)

It's all in the way you look at it.

Unknown

According to Kahneman and Tversky, psychologists who pioneered the Nobel Prize-winning research on integration of decision-making concepts into economics, a frame is "the decision-maker's conception of the acts, outcomes, and contingencies associated with a particular choice[7]."

As we discussed earlier, in many cases, a situation *imposes* a frame of reference, and a decision maker "falls" into this frame, which may allow only certain options as solutions. In essence, you "become framed" right there and then, as the following examples demonstrate.

EXAMPLE 3-4: DAN—THE EPA ULTIMATUM

Dan is the CEO of a manufacturing company. One day, the Environmental Protection Agency (EPA) comes in and gives him an ultimatum: "Either you clean up your plant, or it will be shut down." This plant is the main production plant in the business where the company's core products are manufactured. Other plants do not have the capability to take on this production. The plant has passed environmental inspections without problems in previous years. The plant's closure may mean major difficulties (financial and operational) for the business.

Dan knows that the cleanup is cost-prohibitive, and he cannot allow the shutdown of the plant. As a result, he "falls" into the only option that appears reasonable to him—build a new plant. This solution necessitates borrowing money, which his company does. However, when the economy slows and revenues go down dramatically, the business cannot service the debt and eventually files for bankruptcy protection.

Initially, during the interview, Dan stated the difficulty of this decision: "The whole situation was adversarial from the beginning. We were not given an opportunity to discuss the situation, and we were given an ultimatum to resolve the situation with a very short timeline. We had to act. Building a new plant seemed the best alternative."

Were there other options? Yes. Shortly after the new plant construction started, his company acquired another business with production facilities that could have accommodated the production volume of his main plant and provided the educated labor to do it. Therefore, in theory, the company could have looked for such acquisitions when faced with the initial EPA dilemma.

A decision objective defined too narrowly is another very common way to become "framed," as the following example shows.

EXAMPLE 3-5: KEITH—PLANT CONSOLIDATION

Keith is the CEO of a manufacturing company that has grown partially through acquisitions. As a result, the company has more plants around the world than it would have, had it grown organically. Just recently, Keith put together a team with an objective of optimizing operations within a particular segment of the company that includes four plants. A scenario was proposed in which the company would consolidate three plants into two within this business segment. Such a consolidation would necessitate a closure of the California plant, which has a high cost of exit. The difficulty of the decision about the closure of the California plant is twofold. On one hand, the plant is on the brink of profitability and has good operational people. On the other hand, the market for the company's products in California is uncertain. Last year, however, the company had several large deals that did not materialize but that would have brought significant revenue to the California plant.

Keith decided to take a more detailed look at the California plant before making the consolidation decision. The objective that Keith posed to the team was very clear: "Find ways to achieve the following at the California plant: stop cash drain by the end of the year, and achieve profitable growth within 18 months."

The team brought back a recommendation—keep the plant. The reasoning was based on market growth assumptions and the non-variable costs to operate the plant. The team felt that California was a good market for the company. It also proposed a scenario that would bring the plant to a break-even situation by the end of the year. However, the proposed future profitable growth scenarios were weak in Keith's judgment. Keith listened to the team's report and is contemplating the decision.

It so happens that a competitor approached Keith's company recently with a proposal to buy plants in two business segments that the company serves. The proposal did not include the business segment to which the California plant belongs. The company decided to decline the proposal. However, Keith's thoughts went in the direction of a divesture of this particular segment: He thinks, "The segment is not strategic; we are not making that much money in it, and we do not have a great sales force supporting this segment." He immediately comes up with several buyer candidates that would be very interested in buying the plants in this segment. As he continues this train of thought, his mood changes to excitement—"This is a great idea!"

In his contemplation, Keith realizes that he looked at the whole situation too narrowly. From this broader strategic perspective, the California plant should be closed, and then the segment should be shopped around for a buyer. His reasoning for the closure is that all competitors are ingrained in the California market, and this is one of the reasons Keith's company is having a hard time selling there. It doesn't want this particular plant, but it could greatly benefit from having the others. He now believes that he formulated both objectives too narrowly—the initial objective for the segment operations optimization team and then the objective for the second team to look for ways to make the California plant profitable. He says, "We should have looked at it strategically to begin with!"

As you can see, clarity of perspective is very important in reaching the right decision. Finding the right angle of looking at the problem can open additional options or provide ways to look at the current options in a different light.

The problem, of course, is that when a decision maker is "framed," he or she is usually not aware of this fact. In my work with decision makers on their current business decisions, we utilized the Clarity State to identify a current decision frame and develop alternative frames. In over 30 percent of business decision cases, decision makers found a different perspective or a new frame while contemplating their current decisions in the Clarity State by utilizing the technique described in this book. Chapter 10, "Everything Is Relative!—Why the Right Frame Is Critical," and Chapter 11, "Becoming a Frame Artist—How to Master Clarity of Perspective," present strategies that decision makers found effective in working with frames.

Exercise

Recollect a past decision experience when reconsidering the situation from a different perspective enabled you to find the right solution. How effective are you in identifying and shifting perspectives? Do you do it routinely for most decisions? Rate your performance.

Write down the decision you just remembered, and note whether learning to identify additional perspectives would improve your decision-making.

Difficulty in Selecting Among Options

In each action we must look beyond the action at our past, present, and future state, and at others whom it affects, and see the relations of all those things. And then we shall be very cautious.

Pascal[8]

Most decisions do not have many options. However, often a decision maker is faced with several options that are all possible and potentially good courses of action, as in the following example. On the other hand, sometimes the choices are all "terrible." Finding a way to choose the right path becomes a daunting task.

EXAMPLE 3-6: JACK—SELECTING A WAY TO TRANSITION TO A NEW TECHNOLOGY PLATFORM

Jack is the CEO of a company (MP) that was spun off from the parent several years ago. MP took with it software applications that were developed on an older hardware platform. The market for these applications was gradually moving to the Microsoft software platform. Jack was aware that security and industry analysts were expecting MP to have applications on that platform as well. The decision was pressing. The company needed to find the best way to move to a new development platform and find the right timing for a switch to this new technology.

Three options were open:

- Convert existing applications.
- Develop new applications from scratch based on the existing functionality.
- Abandon internal development and acquire a company with products on the right platform.

All options were feasible and achievable. The product suite consisted of 12 million lines of code that matured over 22 years into 52 applications. These products were very stable. Customers considered the toolset extremely reliable and deep in functionality.

The fastest way was to convert existing applications. The problem with that option was that as with any software that was developed over a long period of time, it had issues buried in it that would have been difficult, if not impossible, to convert. Developing new applications from scratch, on the other hand, was time- and cost-prohibitive. As a result, Jack and his team were looking for a balance between the first two options.

The third option, acquiring a company with a product suite on the right platform, had its own issues. From the information that was publicly available about potential acquisition candidates, none of the software packages that could have been bought in an acquisition provided the depth and breadth of the functionality of MP's existing applications. Therefore, this solution would have to have been amended by either continuing to develop existing applications on the old platform or combining the needed functionality on the new platform over time. Proceeding with an acquisition and also spending money on expanding the acquired software with the needed functionality made this option the most expensive solution. The speed to market was its main advantage, however.

The company spent 18 months making this decision. During this time, a lot of data was collected. MP reviewed what other companies in the industry had done, experimented with various toolsets to perform semiautomatic conversion of the existing applications, and talked to analysts and customers. At this point, MP has selected a toolset and has started converting existing applications.

After much thinking and talking with his team, Jack's decision is to abandon the conversion and the internal development effort and to acquire a company with a proven set of applications on a new platform. At this time, the selected conversion tool is working; 13 of 52 applications are converted and functional. The "development from scratch" team rewrote two applications and timed such development. MP has screened the market for potential acquisition targets.

During the interview, Jack assessed this decision difficulty: "This was a make-or-break decision for the company. The stakes were high, and yet

I was not sure how to proceed. I spent countless hours thinking and talking to people about it."

Jack remembers the moment when this decision became clear to him. He realized that the crux of the issue was that he needed to focus on ways to attract new customers and satisfy their needs. It's not that existing customers were not important; they were, but there were ways to bridge them to the new platform. If the company could not attract new customers quickly, it would start losing market share. As soon as he focused on this critical parameter, a solution became clear.

As you will see later, one of the ways to select an option from among a number of good or bad options is to find the crux of the issue, as Jack did in this example. Identifying a crux usually points you to the right solution instantly.

I discuss how Clarity State can be instrumental in identifying such a crux—or a critical parameter—in a decision in Chapter 11. I use Jack's decision and other similar cases in Appendix B, "Additional Tips on Reducing Decision Complexity," to demonstrate how such complex decisions can be made simpler by creating decision layers. Chapter 12, "Bull's-eye!—How to Align with the Right Outcome," is devoted to techniques of utilizing the Clarity State for selecting the right solution option.

Exercise

Recollect a past decision experience when you had a number of viable options to pursue but the decision was not clear. Looking back at the situation, what was the impetus for the eventual decision? How did you reach clarity? Write down the decision you just remembered and the specific way you reached clarity.

Table 3-1 shows the causes of decision difficulty by the frequency of occurrence in the sample of 115 business decision cases gathered from CEOs during interviews.

TABLE 3-1

Types of decision difficulty prioritized by the frequency of occurrence

Priority	Types of Difficulty	Occurrence (%)
1	Lack of a clear perspective	30%
2	Lack of a clear objective	25%
3	Difficulty in selecting from among options	17%
4	Lack of clear constraints	15%
5	Difficulty in dealing with emotions	13%

During interviews, as I was asking decision makers to discuss their difficult decisions, I also asked questions about how they usually overcome such difficulties. I asked them many questions, including how they deal with emotions, what they do to generate more options, how they identify the main objective, and how they resolve the situation when something is bothering them about the decision but they do not know what it is.

Exercise

Review your notes about past decisions and difficulties associated with them. Compile a table similar to Table 3-1 utilizing the past decisions that you recollected while reading this chapter. What is the most common decision difficulty for you based on this limited probe into your past decision-making?

The innovative ways that decision makers devised for overcoming decision difficulties and making difficult decisions collected during interviews were built into the Clarity State Decision-Making technique that you consider in the next chapter.

CHAPTER 4

How Do You Make Decisions? Overview of a CEO-Tested Process

*The conventional wisdom is that revolutionary ideas come to people after they contemplate a situation, condition, or problem for a long time ... But these observations are trite and not very helpful because coming up with a revolutionary idea is not simply a matter of thinking a long time ... The key is **how** you are thinking about a problem for a long time.*

Guy Kawasaki[1]

Exercise

What is your decision-making process? Who taught you this process? How effective is it? How often do you think about it?

We learn the basics of decision-making by rote early in our lives. We then run our lives with these methods without giving them any serious thought. Very rarely do people decide mindfully how they will make decisions. With time, these basics become ingrained in our decision-making style—frequently depriving us of the ability to look at a situation in new ways.

Our innate decision-making methods often suggest a solution, but because we do not fully "buy it," we continue to think about it, letting the circumstances or someone else make the decision for us. I have seen whole companies in this limbo mode because the leader was unwilling or unable to make a major strategic decision. When we get into such situations, we rarely know why, not to mention knowing ways to get out of it and make a decision with clarity.

Seeing clearly often requires a shift to a more mindful awareness of the situation involved in the decision[2,3]. But telling yourself "Be aware," "Be mindful," or "Shift to a different perspective" does not help. At all times it is better to have a method.

The technique that I am about to share with you which I call *Clarity State Decision-Making*, enables decision makers to make this shift to mindfulness successfully. It is a decision-making process aided by the Clarity State that helps you overcome the five areas of decision difficulty discussed in Chapter 3, "Five Hurdles to Clarity." The main methods of overcoming these difficulties are simple and can be captured in one word each:

> **To overcome Difficulty #1 (lack of a clear objective) and Difficulty #2 (lack of clear constraints), you need to *define* objective and constraints.**

> **To overcome Difficulty #3 (difficulty in dealing with emotions), you need to *detach* from emotions.**

To overcome Difficulty #4 (lack of a clear perspective/ frame), you need to *expand* your view.

To overcome Difficulty #5 (difficulty in selecting among options), you need to *align* yourself with a solution.

The problem, of course, is in the *how*—how do you define the objective and constraints, how do you detach from emotions, how do you expand your perspective, and how do you align with the solution? This is the topic of the rest of the book.

The *Clarity State Decision-Making Process* is based on best practices of overcoming decision difficulties. It also incorporates the results of experimentation with the order and the way that these best practices should be utilized in the Clarity State. The process consists of five parts closely following the resolution of the five types of decision difficulties. It is shown in Figure 4-1.

Parts I—Reach and maintain the Clarity State. Utilizing breathing and mind-focusing techniques, reach a coherent state of mind, body, and emotions quickly and at will, whenever you need to make a decision.

Parts II—Define the decision. Create a one-page decision map that captures the most salient factors related to the decision at the right level of detail.

Parts III—Deal with emotions. Identify, acknowledge, and utilize emotions related to the decision to clarify the issues involved.

Parts IV—Achieve clarity of perspective. Utilize several techniques, like constraints relaxation and others, to identify, evaluate, and select the right way to look at the decision.

Parts V—Align with outcomes. Reflect on the solution options in turn in such a way so that it becomes clear that one option is the right solution.

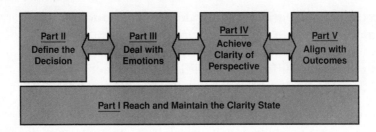

FIGURE 4-1
Clarity State Decision-Making Process

All parts of the process are important. If the decision to be made is not well defined, you might not see the issues clearly and might reach a wrong decision. If you remain in a stressed, unbalanced state of mind and body, it is unlikely that you can reach total alignment with a solution. Or, if you block intuitive reaction to questions while in the Clarity State or rationalize them, you will block a way to the "right" decision.

I also observed that this decision-making process is not linear. Ideas from Part IV (achieving clarity of perspective), for example, can completely change the decision map created in Part II (defining the decision).

Thomas Edison utilized a similar process when he needed to solve a problem with one of his inventions. He would sit in a rocking chair with the formulated problem in mind, rocking slowly and rhythmically while holding a small ball in each hand. He would visualize solutions to the problem. When one of the balls dropped out of his hand, signaling that he had begun to doze, the sound of it hitting the floor would awaken him. Edison would then recall what he had been visualizing at that moment, and more often than not, it was a potential solution to his problem, or at least a step in the right direction.

Similarly, Albert Einstein used to sail a boat while mentally focusing on problems he was trying to solve.

Part I: Reach and Maintain the Clarity State

As the fletcher whittles and makes straight his arrows, so the master directs his straying thoughts.

Gautama Buddha[4]

In 50 percent of cases in my interviews, executives reached the Clarity State in 5 to 10 minutes or less on the first try. With practice, 1 to 3 minutes is sufficient for this step. Attainment of this coherent state can be measured by off-the-shelf software applications, a number of which are available on the market. The software that was used in this project is discussed in detail in Chapter 5, "You Too Can Reach Clarity at Will!—How to Attain the Clarity State." Initially, while you are learning to recognize your own Clarity State, such tools are helpful. With practice, though, you will be able to easily reach Clarity State at any time without the use of software.

Although reaching the Clarity State is not hard, maintaining it while contemplating a tough decision is a challenge; it requires mental discipline and focus that come with practice.

Exercise

Set a timer for 5 minutes. Select an object on your desk or in your current environment. It may be a book, a phone, or a paperweight. Sit quietly in a relaxed position with your eyes closed. Focus on the selected object in your mind's eye until the time is up. During this time, when your mind wanders, bring it back to the object.

You probably noticed that it was not easy to keep your attention on the object. It is even harder when you want to focus on a decision, because there is not even an object to focus on. As a result, keeping attention on a decision is usually a challenge. Mind focusing is an important skill that comes with practice.

I noticed that CEOs who run larger companies are usually better at this skill than others.

Key Point
The better your ability to maintain mental focus, the faster and easier you will reach clarity.

When you are in the Clarity State, the world does not work the same way as it does in your waking life. You have to learn to operate your mind differently. There are several major differences:

- **Trigger**—Remember your clarity moments again. Usually, insights come as "a lot of thoughts together" or "a flash of images, thoughts, and feelings, all combined, very fast." And usually they are triggered by a thought or an image in your mind. Your challenge will be to let your mind "flow" and be open to associations caused by questions and visualizations used in the process so that the trigger is generated.

- **Speed**—The speed of the insight itself is super-fast, but your notion of time seems to slow down in this state. You might have experienced this phenomenon when you are focused on a task and enjoying it—time seems to stop, and you make a lot of progress in much less time than usual. Responses to questions in this state might arrive at a slower pace than you are used to. Your challenge will be to figure out how much time you need to allow for contemplating a question.

- **Interference**—Let me quote one leader who captured the essence of this issue: "There is one thing I learned in the 10 years as a CEO, and that is to trust my instincts more quickly. My mind messes it all up." Unfortunately, this is true—we are quick to override our intuitive reactions. How many interesting thoughts and ideas did you reason away with "I know it can't be true because…"? And this is a skill you need to learn to truly leverage the Clarity State for decision-making—not to override your gut with rational thought, but to listen to it and let the intuitive reaction evolve.

Part II: Define the Decision—Create a Decision Map

No wind serves him who addresses his voyage to no certain port.

Montaigne[5]

Exercise

Describe your *decision definition* method (not the decision-making process)—the way you *define* decisions. State it simply, as if you are teaching a high school class.

How did you do? If you are like most business managers, you do not have a clue about your decision definition method. Why? Because we rarely define our decisions.

Key Point

Many of us want to start with the clarity of action, but the clarity of purpose is the starting point.

The decisions that I worked with executives on were usually strategic and complex. Such decisions usually had interrelationships with other efforts, other strategies, and other unresolved issues within the company. Under such circumstances, it is easy to become lost in the details and not see the forest for the trees.

In my work with decision makers, I found that having a one-page graphical representation of a decision is an extremely effective tool. I call this graphical decision representation a *decision map*.

It served a number of purposes.

First, with the help of the decision map, executives clarified to themselves the problems they were trying to address. The amount of confusion that I observed was staggering!

Second, they had to arrive at the right level of detail in order to represent the most salient factors related to the decision on one page.

Third, since a picture is worth a thousand words, it enabled decision makers to keep this picture in mind while contemplating the decision in the Clarity State.

Figure 4-2 shows a blank decision map.

Decision Map

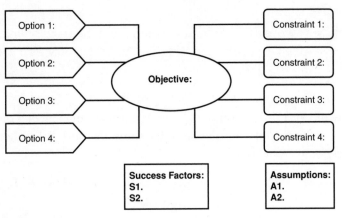

FIGURE 4-2
Decision Map

The power of a simple decision map cannot be underestimated. In many cases, just having such a map generated a "shift" of understanding about the decision and enabled the decision maker to clarify issues related to it. Several executives actually made their decisions after finishing their decision maps and did not need to continue with the rest of the exercise.

You can put together a decision map without using the Clarity State. However, identifying and properly formulating issues related to decision definition sometimes is not easy. We used Clarity State in such cases—when objectives and constraints needed clarification. A specific method of creating a decision map is discussed in Chapter 6, "No Aim, No Game—How to Achieve Clarity of Objective."

Contemplate the Decision—Overcoming Decision Difficulties

Effective executives ... make effective decisions. ... They want to know what the decision is all about and what the underlying realities are which it has to satisfy.

Peter F. Drucker[6]

The objective of the Clarity State Decision-Making Process is to replicate a clarity moment at will and unleash the power of insight on a tough business issue that requires resolution. Another objective is to enable decision makers to use this process by themselves after initial training. However, initially, it was not apparent *how* to use this state for decision-making. I tried several approaches to leverage the Clarity State for decision contemplation after the decision maker completed his or her decision map:

1. Decision makers just contemplated their decisions in the Clarity State without any guidance from me.
2. Decision makers answered questions about their decisions and responded verbally to questions while in the Clarity State.
3. Decision makers silently answered questions about their decisions while in the Clarity State in the time allowed after each question. I asked them to let me know when they were ready to proceed.
4. Decision makers silently answered questions about their decisions in the time allowed after each question. I asked them to tell me when they needed more time to contemplate the answer.

The first method did not work at all. Decision makers reported that they could not stay focused on the decision; their minds wandered to other thoughts, ideas, and problems. The second method was better. However, even though the focus stayed on the decision, people had difficulty maintaining the Clarity State while talking. As a result, the benefits of the Clarity State could not be obtained. Methods three and four were the most successful. Method four was clearly preferred.

Through this experimentation, it became clear that while in the Clarity State, a decision maker needs to be asked questions about the decision in order to focus the mind and help trigger insights. Otherwise, the mind wanders and becomes drawn to other thoughts, ideas, and problems.

Questions asked of decision makers in the last three parts of the process were based on best practices of overcoming decision difficulties, on my own experimentation, and on the feedback from decision makers about the effectiveness of questions to trigger insight and ideas for improving the questions.

The resulting questions are based on all these sources of input; they follow this sequence:

1. Dealing with emotions associated with the decision
2. Achieving clarity of perspective
3. Aligning with outcomes

Part III—Deal with Emotions

We all remember decisions, personal or business, that were emotional. Sometimes the emotion is so strong that a clear decision seems impossible. Yet, conventional wisdom tells us to ignore our emotions—to somehow be "cool" about every situation we encounter. I am sure that you know from experience that this advice does not work. Telling yourself to "be cool" or "ignore it" is not effective.

On the other side of the spectrum, there are situations where we are convinced that we do not have an emotion associated with a decision. Neuroscientists now know that *everything* we do has an underlying emotion associated with it—including every major decision. Meditators will further tell you that every emotion has a specific physical sensation associated with it. We simply are not aware of the emotion or the sensation unless it is extremely strong.

Key Point

Emotions are important inputs about a decision situation that we usually ignore. Working with them effectively can bring clarity to a difficult situation.

I took an unconventional approach to dealing with emotions—asking decision makers to find them, acknowledge them, and use them as tools to reach an emotional balance point. The approach succeeded. As discussed in Chapter 8, "Balancing Mind and Body—How to Learn from Your Emotional Cues," decision makers reported that by using this approach, they discovered sometimes "fascinating" aspects about the contemplated decision or were able to detach from the emotion enough to identify a clear solution.

Part IV: Achieve Clarity of Perspective

We are the prisoners of ideas.

Ralph Waldo Emerson[7]

Clarity moments usually carry with them a shift in perspective—a frame change in which the solution becomes obvious. Without the help of clarity moments, identifying additional perspectives and finding the right one is not a trivial matter.

> ### Exercise
> Imagine that you are buying a business. Or, if you prefer to consider a personal decision, imagine buying something expensive and important to you, like a house. Generate at least three different perspectives of how you might want to look at this decision.

Experienced executives recognize that making a decision within the wrong frame of reference can be extremely dangerous. The decision maker might take false constraints into account or fail to see viable solutions and, as a result, may make a wrong decision or not be able to make a decision at all. In addition, many of the decisions I worked with required detailed and intense computations. It's easy to get "framed" by these details.

Key Point

To reach clarity on a decision faster and easier, make it a practice to look at complex decisions from different frames.

This is easier said than done. And it's all in *how* you do it.

This part of the Clarity State Decision-Making process uses a number of methods to generate alternative frames and enable a decision maker to look at the decision from various angles, eventually finding the perspective that enables clarity, as Jeff did in the following example.

EXAMPLE 4-1: JEFF—EXPANDING INTO NEW MARKETS

Jeff is a CEO and founder of a telecommunications services company focused on a vertical industry segment. His company has grown to become the largest player in this market. Jeff is considering expanding the sales organization to focus on other segments related to the one in which his company has the largest market share.

Jeff is not entirely sure that customers in these market segments will be interested in his company's services. The indications are that they will be. However, without focusing salespeople on it, he cannot be sure. As a result, his desire is to minimize cost exposure. He is also concerned about getting acceptance from his sales team management. It's currently organized by geography, and creating new sales groups focused on specific market segments can be perceived as infringing on their territory and their potential gain—a classic dilemma for a sales organization being organized in a matrix. Discussions with sales management so far have not been conclusive, and Jeff feels resistance.

Here is Jeff's feedback after he went through the technique of Clarity State Decision-Making: "I realized that I am deep in discussions with sales managers optimizing the sales organization while I should be looking at the situation in a completely different way—from a market perspective. What is the most effective way to meet the needs of this market? Which specific segments should we go after? Where is the highest potential? What is the best way to reach these segments? Which ones should we address first? I became furious with myself for not realizing this sooner."

The details of the methods used in this part of the process are discussed in Chapter 10, "Everything Is Relative!—Why the Right Frame Is Critical," and Chapter 11, "Becoming a Frame Artist—How to Master Clarity of Perspective," but here is a brief summary.

First, you give your decision definitions a good "shake-up" in the Clarity State. The result is a cleaner definition—perceived constraints are eliminated, constraints are reworded at a similar level of detail, or decision layers are defined to manage complexity.

Second, you use the technique that I call *constraints relaxation* to generate alternative perspectives. A constraints relaxation exercise challenges decision makers to "stretch" constraints by imagining situations when constraints are absent from the definition or situations where constraints are maximized, thus providing a number of unique frames for looking at the decision. It's like looking at the decision through a microscope where only issues relevant to this constraint are visible; the rest is shaded from view.

Third, having achieved a cleaner definition and a number of fresh perspectives through the constraints relaxation exercise, you visualize your decisions under different circumstances with the objective of expanding your view about the decision.

Key Point

Achieving clarity in a decision often involves seeing a large picture or a longer time frame or finding a bigger perspective. The larger your view, the clearer you can be about your decision.

Decision makers reported that this approach provided fresh ways of looking at their tough situations, either enabling them to make a decision right away or paving the way to a clear decision.

Part V: Align with Outcomes—Visualizing the Future

Fortune sides with him who dares.

Virgil[8]

Strategic decisions always involve uncertainty. Should we diversify through acquisition? Should we commit more funds to a highly promising but still uncertain project or terminate it? Should we commit additional resources to a declining business or milk it?

These are the cases when decision makers summon their intuition and vision power to then base their decisions on the projections of the future. Methods such as evaluating pros and cons, asking for advice, building probability trees, eliminating alternatives, evaluating options relative to a reference point, making trade-offs, and using mind mapping are just methods of *feeding intuition* with data and analysis. The final call is a leader's choice based on the gut feeling of what is right for the business.

Key Point

Vision power is the ability to engage imagination in such a way as to perceive the most likely course of future developments. Leaders have to develop this skill!

The approach I used in this part of the Clarity State Decision-Making process is visualization. I asked decision makers to use their minds in the Clarity State as a playground for their ideas—considering solution options from various angles, imagining the consequences that may follow from each course of action, evaluating key uncertainties, and visualizing the realization of the objective and all constraints. I encouraged them to look for the solution that has the most promise, the one that is in the best alignment with the decision maker. Specific methods are discussed in Chapter 12, "Bull's-eye!—How to Align with the Right Outcome."

The approach worked—most decision makers reported that they were able to clearly find the solution that mentally and emotionally aligned with them. They were able to find the elusive clarity.

The following is an example of an experienced executive who was under pressure from groups in her division to adopt different paths of action. Using the Clarity State Decision-Making technique outlined previously, she was able to find a broader, more constructive perspective that was valuable for her and then reach a clear decision.

EXAMPLE 4-2: MARY—INTERNAL COMPETITION FOR FUNDING

Mary is a division head of a large company in the durable consumer goods sector. Within her division, two groups were competing for funding. One group was working on a plan to consolidate two customer service centers, and the group needed money to fund changes to the customer relationship management system. The other group needed funding for a distribution center for a critical equipment update.

As Mary reflected on the needs, she became convinced that both requests would have to be funded. However, the division could invest only a certain amount of money that year—whatever was in the budget, which was not enough for both projects. Here is Mary's feedback after she went through the Clarity State Decision-Making technique: "I realized that we could fund both projects, but not simultaneously! I decided to immediately fund the distribution center needs. It also became clear how we could shift customer service load to other locations, reap the cost savings that we expected, and utilize these savings in funding the software changes. This was a result that I did not expect!"

Mary shared how she arrived at this conclusion as a result of using the technique. "I had a number of concerns that were real. If we did not act quickly on both projects, our customers would feel it. The decision definition part of the process helped me clarify these concerns. Things started falling into place." Mary was able to identify and work with her emotions: "I found some anxiety associated with the situation. As I focused on it, I realized where it was coming from, and I added another constraint." The constraints relaxation exercise identified a new perspective: "As you were asking me to look at constraints one by one, I found that one constraint in particular was 'framing' me. This constraint focused me on the fact that we committed to the parent company that we would *complete* the customer center's consolidation. But, in reality, we committed to the cost saving *results* that my division was going to deliver, not the actual consolidation."

She finally found her insight trigger: "You asked me to visualize a situation where these problems had been addressed. When I did that and looked at it from a higher perspective and a broader view, I suddenly saw all our customer centers in a map in front of me. It became clear how we could move traffic between them and achieve the cost savings that we were looking for. Everything became clear in an instant. The solution was so simple."

Before I launch into a detailed discussion of specific methods involved in the technique, let us briefly discuss the applicability of this technique to decision-making in companies of various sizes.

Decision-Making in Large Versus Small Companies

The Clarity State Decision-Making technique has worked for executives and leaders of companies of all sizes. You can use it to make a decision, evaluate a proposed path of action, pinpoint a disagreement and resolve it, or a combination of these.

However, the differences between decision-making processes in large and small companies will impact the way this process might be used in companies of different sizes and the parts of the process that become important.

Managers who are actively involved in defining the decision and evaluating it with or without their team's help and with or without outside assistance and advice will use the process to *make a decision* by clarifying objective and constraints, dealing with emotions, evaluating perspectives, and aligning with outcomes.

As decision-making processes mature with a company's size, decision definition and framing are pushed down the organizational structure. A higher-level manager is less involved in the structuring of the decision and is almost never involved in collecting information to evaluate solutions. He or she is usually presented with a proposed path of action on a particular issue with some depth of supporting material with it.

In these situations, an executive has to be able to pierce layers of assumptions, ask the right questions, and come up with various perspectives from which to look at the decision. The good news is that the decision rarely needs to be made on the spot.

The value of the technique in these cases is in using it to *evaluate the proposed path of action*—review the objective, constraints, and assumptions to make sure that the right strategic perspective has been evaluated. In contrast with a manager who is intimately involved in a decision, a manager who is asked to make a decision based on a proposal may use this process to discover a new perspective to take on a decision, areas of concern that have not been fully addressed, or additional questions to be clarified.

In general, it is my observation that CEOs of small and medium companies face more decisions that they consider difficult.

Why?

First of all, in a small company, a CEO relies mostly on himself or herself and close team members. In a large company, a CEO relies on the team as well but also on the rigor of the company's decision-making processes.

Second, due to financial constraints, more decisions in smaller companies end up in the category of "betting the company," whereas in large companies, such occurrences are rare.

As the company's size increases, a *decision-making structure* is introduced, along with a necessary organizational structure. This structure ensures that certain parts of the decision-making process are accomplished properly. These decision-making processes are unique for each company based on its history and evolution, its founders, and the experience of the management team. For example, the level and amount of information collected for a decision might be deeper in comparison with what a small company will do or can afford to do. Or, the depth and rigor of financial projections might be better. In a small company, resources cannot usually be allocated to checking and rechecking assumptions or hiring a consultant with expertise in the field.

Not only do larger companies need formal decision-making structures because of their size, but they also strive to incorporate *best practices* into decision-making that ensure better results. The following list provides several examples of such best practices:

- Provide a way to check and recheck assumptions.
- Encourage various interests within the company and even outside it, if applicable, to participate in the decision. As a result, the process ensures that many perspectives on the issue are heard and evaluated.
- Provide contention on purpose.
- Force a review of "what-if" scenarios for each solution.
- Hire experts in the field to provide deep analysis and opinions on an issue when needed.

The same or similar processes can be introduced into a small company, but they rarely are. As a result, more often than not, a CEO of a small company is forced to go with his "gut" in a decision, thus assuming more risk and having to deal with a bigger emotional load. In a large company setting, decisions are not emotionless, but many aspects that otherwise would have caused emotional response are taken out of consideration. For example, the fear that a certain concern was not fully evaluated will not be there, because someone on the team in a large company was assigned to evaluate this risk. In a small company, this risk was recognized but not evaluated due to the lack of resources.

Too much reliance on the rigor of the decision-making processes in a large company can be a problem as well. CEOs of large companies talk about continuously maintaining the company's decision-making processes in "health" by ensuring that

- Divergent views are not squashed
- Contention is built into the processes
- Interesting and creative ideas are heard and evaluated
- Assumptions are rigorously questioned and evaluated

The Clarity State Decision-Making process benefits managers in companies of all sizes. By adopting this technique, managers in small and large companies alike will create a stronger overall decision-making infrastructure—in smaller companies by adding robust decision definition structure and options evaluation rigor, and in larger companies by providing additional ways to structure and evaluate decisions.

Let us now discuss the parts of the technique in detail.

CHAPTER 5

You Too Can Reach Clarity at Will!—How to Attain the Clarity State

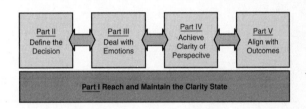

You are searching for the magic key that will unlock the door to the source of power; and yet you have the key in your own hands, and you may make use of it the moment you learn to control your thoughts.

Napoleon Hill[1]

Chapter 2, "The Clarity State—Mental Focus Redefined," defined the Clarity State in the following way:
The Clarity State is the state of being

- *Physically relaxed*
- *Emotionally positive, happy, released from fear and anxiety*
- *Charged with power, success, self-confidence, and energy*
- *Totally in the present*
- *Mentally focused on the task at hand*

Clarity State is a state of physical, emotional, and mental coherence. Another way to describe this state is being at a high point of three scales—physical, emotional, and mental (see Figures 5-1 through 5-3).

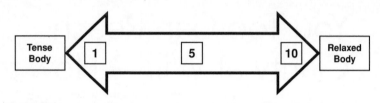

FIGURE 5-1
Physical Scale

On the low point of the physical scale, your body is in fight-or-flight mode—ready to respond to the danger that you sense in the environment. Your bloodstream is full of adrenaline. On the high side of the scale, your body is fully relaxed.

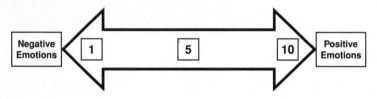

FIGURE 5-2
Emotional Scale

The low point of the emotional scale is when you are under the grip of negative emotions, such as worry, anger, frustration, or envy, or you feel resignation—no interest or ability to influence the world around you. At these times your body produces the hormone cortisol. On the high side of the scale, you feel full of energy, excited about your work, and energetic. At these times your body produces the hormone dehydroepiandrosterone (DHEA), which has been called an "anti-age" hormone.

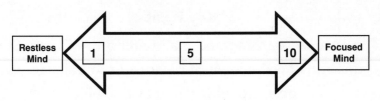

FIGURE 5-3
Mental Scale

At the low point of the mental scale, your thoughts rush from one to another, never stopping to take one concept through to its conclusion. At the high point of the scale, you can focus on one issue to the exclusion of everything else for a period of time, independent of how difficult it is, and make progress in addressing the issue.

All three systems are interconnected. The state of one influences the others. Emotions affect the state of your physical body and your mind, and vice versa.

> **Exercise**
>
> What is your average state during the day? On a scale from 1 (low) to 10 (high), rate your physical, emotional, and mental state. Now, compute your average score across the three scales.

Reaching the Clarity State involves a shift to a high point on each scale. However, a shift on one scale will affect another. A further shift on the other will affect the third, thus increasing your overall average (coherence) score.

You do not need to reach the highest mark on all scales. In fact, successful athletes know that a certain level of stress or anxiety is necessary for optimal performance. This is based on the theory of optimal arousal pioneered by Yuri Hanin, a sports psychologist from the former USSR, and now accepted by sports psychologists worldwide[2]. Successful athletes have learned how to maintain the arousal level within a certain optimal zone and to constructively channel the energy that the anxiety generates. On a scale from 1 (low) to 10 (high), shoot for an average coherence level of 7 or 8.

Key Point

The ease of reaching and maintaining the Clarity State depends on the level of balance or imbalance you operate under in your daily life.

If you usually operate at a coherence level of around 3, the shift to 8 will be harder in comparison with a person who usually operates around 6. The good news is that you can change your state at will, any time you want to, or whenever you have a difficult decision to make. The second piece of good news is that you can do it rather quickly, within 5 to 10 minutes. Obviously, if you are under exceptional stress, you might need extra time to shift to the Clarity State. Another piece of good news is that the process of reaching the Clarity State is relatively simple, and a lot of methods will work.

In general, as with any skill, your initial attempts might take longer, but with practice, 1 to 3 minutes should be sufficient to get to the Clarity State. I base this statement on feedback from decision makers who decided to incorporate this technique into their daily decision-making process.

Measuring the Attainment of the Clarity State

Each one of us knows this state and has been in it many times. However, if you normally operate at coherence level 2, you are used to this low state. From this vantage point, having reached a slightly higher state, say 5, you might assume that you have reached your Clarity State. An objective indicator can be helpful during the initial learning stage. It can help you *recognize your Clarity State*. Later, as you learn to reach it consistently, you will be able to get into it any time you need to with or without the help of an indicator.

A number of off-the-shelf tools can be used for this purpose. In my research project, I used the Freeze-Framer software from HeartMath, Inc.[3] as a measurement tool for attainment of the Clarity State. The Freeze-Framer software package uses information from a fingertip pulse sensor that plugs into a computer to provide real-time information about your mind-body-emotions state and to indicate when you have achieved a state of autonomic nervous system balance.

The software is based on 20 years of research by HeartMath and is used by many companies around the world. It is intended to help a person shift from a "stressed" state to a coherent state. Over the last 20 years, HeartMath has documented numerous studies proving that shifting to a higher coherence state several times a day for just a couple of minutes has a dramatic impact on improving health, job performance, and overall perception of life[4].

Here are a couple of documented physiological impacts:

- After a month of practicing, the experimental group demonstrated an average 23% reduction in cortisol levels and a 100% increase in DHEA.

- Practicing shifting to a higher coherence level led to changes in the brain's information processing capabilities that result in significant gains in cognitive performance. In one study, high school students in the program demonstrated a 35% mean gain in their math test scores. The mean gain in reading was 14%. Several students were able to increase their test scores by more than 75% after the three-week program.

- A 5-minute experience of positive emotions produced an immediate, significant increase in S-IgA levels. S-IgA is secretory immunoglobulin A, the predominant antibody that serves as the body's first line of defense against infection. In contrast, as a result of a 5-minute experience of a negative emotion such as anger, S-IgA levels dropped sharply in the hour after the anger episode and remained significantly suppressed for *five hours after the initial 5-minute emotional experience.*

I used the tool for confirming the attainment of a higher coherence level before the start of decision contemplation phases of the technique. The tool was also used for making sure that a decision maker maintains the state during decision contemplation (more on this in a minute).

Learning Your Clarity State—A Five-Step Process

> *The disciplined man masters thoughts by stillness and*
> *emotions by calmness.*
> *Lao-Tzu*[5]

The technique of *Reaching the Clarity State* is a stepping function, consisting of five steps, as shown in Figure 5-4. *By using this technique, you are consciously shifting your state to a higher state of coherence.* You start by shifting your position higher on the physical scale by relaxing your body. You then shift your position on the mental scale by using your mind to achieve higher concentration. This shift positively impacts your emotional state by calming your emotions and improves your physical state by further calming and relaxing your body. In the final step, you make a shift on the emotional scale that brings up your overall coherence level again. By shifting to a higher state of coherence, you can clear away the mass of encumbering thought material so that you may bring it into plain view and focus on the issue at hand.

FIGURE 5-4
Reaching the Clarity State Process

Several methods can be utilized for each step. I will first provide brief descriptions of such methods. You will have to experiment with them and identify the ones that work for you in each step. I will then present the technique of reaching the Clarity State that has preselected methods for each step. This technique worked for most decision makers who participated in the project and was found effective in helping them quickly achieve the Clarity State.

Prepare—Methods for Step 1

Find a quiet place where you will not be disturbed. Make sure that phones are turned off. It is better to sit in a comfortable chair with a straight back. You want to be in a relaxed position. The position, however, should not be too comfortable. Otherwise, you run the risk of falling asleep.

Clean off the table surface in front of you, leaving only a sheet of paper and a pen—you might want to write down interesting ideas that occur to you during the exercise. Tell yourself that you are ready to experiment and have fun with the exercise.

Initially, until you learn the process well and can get into the Clarity State within minutes, keep your eyes closed during the exercise. This makes you focus better. Closing your eyes and looking up about 20 degrees behind your eyelids will help you relax and focus easier as well.

Physical Relaxation—Methods for Step 2

Progressive Relaxation

Relax your muscles, progressing slowly from your feet to your calves, thighs, abdomen, chest, lower back, upper back, shoulders, hands, arms, neck, and head, saying to yourself as you do so: "The muscles of my _____ are becoming relaxed and heavy" for every part of your body that you are working on. Feel your body totally relax.

Full Breathing

Start breathing deeply using full breaths in the yoga tradition[6] (inhaling with the abdomen first as it gets pulled in, then with the chest and then the shoulders, exhaling in the reverse order, with the abdomen muscles relaxing at the end of the breath cycle). Do not try to hold your breath. Assume a rhythm that is comfortable for you. Try the rhythm of inhaling for 4 seconds and exhaling for 8. Then experiment with finding your own rhythm. Usually, exhaling should be double the duration of inhaling. Totally focus on your breath. The number of full breaths that you need to reach relaxation depends on your state of mind. If you are in a reasonably relaxed state already, you might need just a couple of full breaths. If you are tense and stressed, you will need tens of full breaths to reach a solid relaxation level.

Calm Your Mind—Methods for Step 3

Relaxation Response[7]

Pick a word, sound, or phrase that has meaning for you. Breathe slowly and naturally, and as you do, say this focus word, sound, or phrase silently to yourself as you exhale. Any word will do; you can use "one" or "relax."

Assume a passive attitude. Don't worry about how well you are doing. When other thoughts come to mind, simply say to yourself, "Oh, well," and gently return to your repetition.

Continue for several minutes. Depending on your current state of mind, you will need from 5 to 20 minutes to reach a relaxed, focused state of mind.

Countdown[8]

Initially, this practice is recommended for the morning or evening, right after you wake up or before you drift off to sleep, because it is known that the relaxed and focused state of mind is easier to achieve at that time. When you have experienced this state and have learned to get into it with a brief countdown, you can do it any time during the day.

When you awaken in the morning, set your alarm for 15 minutes in case you drift off to sleep during the exercise. Now, slowly, at about 2-second intervals, count backward from 100 to 1. As you do this, keep your mind on it. After you practice this countdown for a week, do a 50 to 1 countdown for a week, then 25 to 1, and so on until you get to a relaxed state in a 5 to 1 countdown.

Clear Your Mind—Methods for Step 4

Acknowledging Your Thoughts[9]

Tell yourself, "I feel totally fine and joyful about how life is going." Most likely a thought or an unsolved issue will pop up in your mind that says "not so." It might or might not be related to the issue you wanted to deal with. Acknowledge it; say, "*Yes, that's there.*" Don't get involved with it; just acknowledge it. Imagine that this issue is a block and you are putting it down beside you on the floor. Now tell to yourself, "Other than this issue, I feel totally fine and joyful about how life is going." Continue stacking your unsolved issues on top of each other as you name them. When you have a sufficient stack of blocks, move them to the side.

It is as if you are clearing a space within your mind to devote your attention to the issue at hand. As another analogy, it is as if you come to a pond that is full of algae on the surface, and you clear a part of the surface close to the shore so that you can go for a swim.

The issue in question will probably surface, too; put it aside as well. When no other issues appear, you are ready to proceed to the next step. Or you might sit quietly and enjoy this state for a little while.

Visualization[10,11]

Imagine that you are surrounded by a large sphere of light. When a thought pops into your mind, put it outside of this sphere. Continue doing this until the speed with which you encounter thoughts slows down or you reach a state of no thoughts.

Charge Up—Methods for Step 5

Activating a Symbol

Find an image or images that symbolize power, force, and energy for you. For example, I get this feeling of self-power, force, and energy surging through me when I am standing in front of a stormy ocean. I also get it in the mountains when I am totally in awe of nature's magnificence. Also, several pictures of my past successes with a definite feeling of "it was a challenge and I did it" invoke the same feeling in me. Find your own pictures and images.

Utilize Your Volitional Factors[10]

Identify your volitional (intrinsically motivational) factors, and learn how to use them in converting situations from negative to positive. Here is the process of identifying your volitional factors.

Recollect a moment when you experienced great happiness or exhilaration in something you did. The ideal choice is the event or achievement you recall as being *among the most exciting, the most satisfying, and requiring the greatest investment of effort on your part.* Do not discard the experiences that you believed were "easy" to achieve. You might have been in exactly the right state while you were in the process of achieving them, enjoying the process, and this is why they felt easy. However, they did require effort on your part. Pick three such events.

For each event, put together a separate cluster using the following three steps. Start by writing the name of the event in the middle of a piece of paper, and then circle it. For every word or phrase that you put down during this process, circle it and connect it to other circles on the page. Do not think; just write and associate freely.

● Imagine that the event is happening again. Recall the thoughts and feelings that went through your mind. Write them down, circle them and connect them to other circles.

● Ask yourself what things have contributed to this peak experience. Consider books, people you admire, friends who supported you— anything significant that was a contributing factor. Write them down, circle them, and connect them to other circles.

● Now focus on things that you did directly and deliberately to ac- complish this event. Note any details about your education or em- ployment history that were instrumental. Write them down, circle them and connect them to other circles.

Now look at these three clusters and find similar or identical factors across the three clusters that are particularly important and exciting for you in these situations. You'll find that these factors are the highly mo- tivational factors for you in general; they are your "drivers"—they help you achieve peak performance in your life.

For example, the following themes carry high motivational content for me and surfaced in my clusters:

● This is a great challenge and I did it!

● This is so exciting! This is something new ahead, and I can learn new things!

● This is an opportunity where I can learn from the best, and I can be better than the best!

You can see that my motivational factors are challenges that have nov- elty, variety, and difficulty.

After you figure out your volitional factors, you can use them to convert negative feelings into positive ones, such as fear into excitement. Here is how I use them. In a situation that is a "drag," I find a way to look at it in such a way that it represents a challenge, an opportunity to learn something new, and an opportunity to conquer the odds.

After experimenting with these methods, I found the following combination of breathing and visualization to be the easiest and fastest way to reach the Clarity State that worked for most decision makers. You should select a preferred method that works for you. The objective is to recognize your own Clarity State and learn a simple way to get there quickly and easily.

Recommended Technique for Reaching the Clarity State

Step 1: Prepare.

- Sit quietly in a comfortable position, preferably with your back straight.
- Close your eyes and look up about 20 degrees behind your eyelids. This helps you relax and focus easier.

Step 2: Relax your body.

- Start breathing deeply and slowly. It should feel like a sigh on the exhale. Imagine that the tension is coming out of you with each exhale.
- Scan your body, and if you find tension anywhere, breathe through this tension and relax it.

Step 3: Calm your mind.

- Pick a word, sound, or phrase such as "relax," and say it to yourself on the exhale.

Step 4: Clear your mind.

- When thoughts arrive, do not get involved with them; simply say "I'll deal with it later" and return to your breathing and repetition.

Step 5: Charge up.

- You are now relaxed and focused on your breathing. Let's add a positive charge to this state. Recall a situation when you felt totally happy. Re-experience it with as many senses as possible. If you are on the beach, feel the sun on your skin and your toes in the sand.

- Now recall an experience where you felt very successful, self-confident, excited, on top of the world, with a "no barriers exist for me" feeling. Relive it as vividly as possible with as many senses involved as possible. Get into this feeling of excitement, self-power, and success.

During interviews, this technique flow was read to decision makers with the appropriate intervals between instructions. If you decide to do it on your own, record the steps on a tape and play them back to yourself. You can monitor your progress with software such as Freeze-Framer and experiment with the best way for you to reach the state of coherence.

With practice, you can get to a point where you can program this state to a trigger and get into Clarity State within seconds, as discussed next.

Programming a Clarity State Trigger

When you reach a point where you can consistently reach your Clarity State, you can "program" this state of your body, mind, and emotions to a trigger. Here is the process.

Pick a sign that you will use to trigger this state. The trigger can be bringing together the thumb and first two fingers of either hand, saying to yourself, "One, two, three," or whatever trigger you define. Suppose you pick "One, two, three" for the trigger. Next time you reach Clarity State, say to yourself silently or aloud, "Whenever I say 'One, two, three' silently to myself, I will instantly reach this level of mind to accomplish whatever I focus on."

Practice this daily (three to five times a day) for about a week, always using the same words so that your mind develops a firm association between your trigger and this state.

Using Clarity State for Decision-Making

As far as your self-control goes, as far goes your freedom.
Marie von Ebner-Eschenbach[12]

Reaching Clarity State is simple, but maintaining it for decision-making is not as easy.

Why? Because difficult decisions usually involve issues that are serious, important, and potentially emotional for a decision maker. You may snap out of the desired state the minute you introduce the decision situation into your consciousness. Just one thought, and you are out!

Therefore, this step requires practice and concentration. This is where learning to discipline and focus your mind becomes very important. You cannot always control your circumstances, but you can control your own thoughts.

Exercise

Reach the Clarity State. Now *slowly* bring into your mind the problem or decision you need to make. Do not think about it. You are looking for a state where the problem is there with all its aspects, people, conflicts, financial projections, and "all that" in your mind, and you are considering it but not thinking about it rationally.

Make sure that as you introduce the issue or decision into your consciousness, you are maintaining the Clarity State. Stay with this for a minute or so.

You will need to maintain and monitor your relaxed, positively charged state *and* be able to contemplate your decision. As you experiment with this, you will notice that your attention is in a "parallel" mode: monitoring your state as well as contemplating your decision. As you try it, I am sure that you will find it challenging, requiring a much higher mental focus than normal. Use the Freeze-Framer or a similar program to monitor your state as you are experimenting. With practice, you will quickly notice when you are "dropping the state" and will find easy ways to get back to it quickly.

The reason I am using the verb "contemplate" rather than "think about" in "contemplate a decision" is because your objective is to balance the intuitive and the rational and *not* think in your normal way. It is as if you are putting your rational thinking into the background and getting your intuitive thinking to step forward to give you a reaction to all the rationales you are considering. Again, as you try this, you will find that it is not easy, either. We condition our minds to respond with preset thoughts and rationalize new and interesting ideas out of consideration. Allowing these new ideas and insights into our minds requires mental flexibility and a higher-than-normal level of mental observation.

You also need to focus your mind totally and completely on the decision to the exclusion of everything else. Total and complete focus! It is as if your decision is in a spotlight, and everything else is in the dark. Unfortunately, this is easier said than done. You will find as you try it that thoughts unrelated to your decision will intervene and your attention will be diverted to other things. Maintaining total and complete focus on your decision is a challenging task requiring a high level of mental discipline and control.

This ability to sharply and quickly focus the mind on an issue must be developed with experience. I believe that the larger the company a CEO runs, the more developed this ability becomes.

I remember one example. I was scheduled to go on a trip to interview a CEO of a multibillion Fortune 50 company. The interview was scheduled to take two hours. The CEO's secretary called a couple of days before the interview and informed me that there would be an emergency board meeting right after the interview and asked me to finish the interview a little earlier. Obviously, I agreed. However, as I was getting on a plane to fly to the interview, I have to admit that I was wondering whether this trip would be worth my time. I was concerned about this CEO's ability to really focus on the interview in light of the upcoming emergency board meeting.

The mental focus, mind control, and discipline that this CEO exhibited amazed me. He was in control, able to quickly focus his mind, and able to get into the relaxed and positive state within a couple minutes. Not to mention that he gave me his full attention.

Not to overly generalize, but I do correlate this ability of mental control to the level of achievement a person can reach. Success and concentration—the ability to bend all your energies to one point and go directly to that point—go hand in hand. Therefore, the effort of finding your Clarity State and learning to use it for decision-making can pay handsomely over time.

To summarize, a number of behavior guidance rules are useful to know before you use Clarity State Decision-Making.

Behavior Guidance Points

1. *Maintain your state at all times.*

    It is useful to find a method that enables you to return to the Clarity State quickly if you notice that you are no longer there. Keep a cue on it at all times while focusing on your decision. I suggest using breathing as your cue and as a refocusing mechanism. One part of your attention should keep a cue on your breathing and another on contemplating a decision. If you are getting too deeply involved in the issue or getting emotional, return to just maintaining the Clarity State. Doing a couple of full, deep breaths will refocus you on your state.

2. *Do not worry how well you are doing. Treat this exercise as a game.*

    I found that because business executives are competitive by nature, many of them wanted to get to an even better state, as indicated by the software, in essence competing with the program. This is the wrong focus! The focus should be on maintaining the state and focusing the mind on the decision itself.

    It is important to develop an "it's a game" attitude. The basketball coach Stan Kellner observed: "The player who thinks too much while playing inhibits himself. A player needs to learn to 'let it happen' rather than trying to 'make it happen.'"

3. *Do not rush to provide answers to questions from your rational mind.*

    As stated already, this is not our normal rational thinking process. It usually takes a couple of seconds after the question for the intuitive answer to form. Just wait a couple of seconds.

4. *Be open to insights.*

    Remember that this process is focused on triggering insights. Do not worry if you do not have any associations in response to a particular question; it's okay. Just listen and let it go. The answer might come back later in association with something else or not at all. In cases when you do get an association in response to a question, make sure that you allow it to play out. As we've discussed before, insights may come as pictures, thoughts, images, or ideas. They may all come together in a flash. Allow these ideas to sink in.

PART I

5. *Be observant and precise.*

   The feedback about an issue related to the decision might not come in the form of a thought but rather as an emotion—resistance to a path of action, for example. Or, it may come as a physical sensation. You have to watch for all of these thoughts, emotions, and sensations in your body. They are there to give you information about something related to your decision. When you see something new about your decision, a new perspective, an additional constraint, or other things, be as precise as possible in identifying it. This is very important in order to get additional clarity for your decision.

6. *Maintain complete and total focus on the issue at hand.*

   As discussed before, this rule is the most challenging, because many issues and other decisions are competing for your attention. Thoughts related to these issues *will* interfere with your contemplation. This is why I decided to ask decision makers to silently answer questions about their decision rather than allow them to contemplate it in a free form. Questions focus your mind on the decision. It is likely, however, that other thoughts will still interfere. When they do, simply return the focus of your attention to the contemplation of your decision.

The following chapters discuss various techniques that I've used with decision makers in overcoming decision difficulties while they contemplated their current decision in the Clarity State. I've found that in many cases, being in the Clarity State facilitated a breakthrough in their thinking about the situation related to a decision, enabling them to overcome the difficulties and come to a clear choice.

Practice

Practice maintaining the Clarity State while having an issue in your mind. You might start with focusing on an object rather than a difficult issue. When unrelated thoughts interfere, bring your attention back to the object or issue. Maintain this state for 1 to 3 minutes.

CHAPTER 6

No Aim, No Game— How to Achieve Clarity of Objective

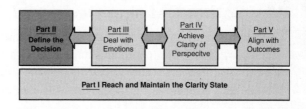

Our plans miscarry because they have no aim. When a man does not know what harbor he is making for, no wind is the right wind.

Seneca[1]

Using Clarity State on your decision is like shining a powerful light on a dark spot. But if you do not know what you intend to find in this dark spot, having this powerful light will not help you. Similarly, the Clarity State will not help you come to a resolution on a decision if you do not know what the problem is.

Remember this dialog from *Alice's Adventures in Wonderland*[2]?

Alice: "Would you tell me, please, which way I ought to go from here?"

Cheshire-Cat: "That depends a good deal on where you want to get to."

Alice: "I don't much care where…"

Cheshire-Cat: "Then it doesn't matter which way you walk."

Too often in our haste and impatience to get going with the implementation, we do not allow ourselves sufficient time to define decisions. We just pick an alternative and get going. In many cases we are going the wrong way at great speed without realizing it!

Key Point

Effective executives define decisions.

Most managers do not.

Why Bother Defining Decisions?

What happens when we do not define a decision?

Usually, after we implement a haphazardly selected solution, we are surprised at the result—that it is different from what we expected and wanted. As a consequence, much valuable time that could have been spent in achieving the initial business objective is lost, not to mention the wasted energy and other resources. Very frustrating! In addition, we have to put more time and resources into implementing another solution.

Let's take two examples of a similar decision in two different companies. Both companies are start-ups that have grown to several million dollars in revenue and are at a point in their development when a professional management team needs to be put in place. Both are starting with the first major position to fill—the VP of Sales. Let's examine the differences of how these companies went about selecting a candidate for the position.

EXAMPLE 6-1: COMPANY A—HIRING A VP OF SALES

Company A has bootstrapped itself, is profitable, and has accumulated some reserve money. However, at the time of the decision, the company has been losing money for the last three months, making the founders (Tom and Steve) uncomfortable and making them question the timing of the decision.

Tom and Steve spent a lot of time interviewing candidates. They also spent money to hire a recruiter in order to identify a good candidate. The finalist was a mature, experienced individual from their industry who, they felt, could do the job. One of the important factors that Tom and Steve focused on was the candidate's ability to put together a sales strategy for the company and then assemble a team to execute the strategy. Tom interviewed the finalist at least 10 times. To this day, he cannot say what was bothering him, but something was.

Very shortly after the person was hired, it became clear to Tom that he was not performing. Tom was wrestling with the question "Should we fire the guy, or are we being too impatient? Have we given him enough time?"

Finally, Tom and Steve decided to talk to the new VP. Together, they developed specific sales group objectives for the next month. Nothing really changed in the new VP's results or approach after the meeting. In Tom's words, "He was approaching his job as if he was in a large company and had tons of time to develop strategy and think about the organizational structure for the future team. But we needed deals, we needed revenue, and this was not happening." Two weeks after the objective-setting meeting, they let the new VP go. The founders reached the conclusion that "The guy talked the right talk, but could not execute."

EXAMPLE 6-2: COMPANY B—HIRING A VP OF SALES

Company B is similar to Company A in its stage of development. Its founders had previously closed all sales deals themselves. The company is not profitable but has recently raised several million dollars in equity from a venture capital firm.

Four people were involved in the interviewing process for a new VP of Sales. They went from 20 candidates to three and then two. Three people were backing one candidate (Jack), and one was backing the other (David). Jack was polished, mature, from the same industry, and a strategist, while David was an aggressive, "hungry" football player, not brilliant strategically. They finally hired David, and, so far, everyone is happy with this selection.

The selection was made based on one factor—the fit between the individual and the company's needs in its stage of development. Even though the team liked the strategist Jack, they realized that the company actually needed the aggressiveness of execution. They were "hungry" for immediate deal closures and more revenue, so a "hungry" David was a better fit. They also realized that David might not remain their VP of Sales as the company grows and enters a more mature stage of development.

What is the difference between these two companies in making a similar decision? The difference is in the clarity of the decision definition—the articulation of an objective and constraints in the case of Company B. Company B knew that they needed fast execution and revenue, and they hired the appropriate candidate. Company A did not define their needs clearly. They were under the impression that they wanted a mature strategist, but when this person focused on developing a strategy, they realized that they needed fast execution first. It is hard to move effectively when you don't know where you are moving or whether you will get there.

Not only did Company A spend time and money in getting to the current disappointing result (it is back to square one), but it also needs to find another VP of Sales, another time-consuming and costly process. This is a very high price to pay for not spending a couple of hours or, at the maximum, a week on defining a decision!

Assignment

The rest of the chapter provides specific methods of identifying and refining decision objectives. As you go through the exercises in this chapter, work on clarifying your decision's objective using the decision you selected in Chapter 1, "The Key to Mastering Decisions," as an example. If you prefer to contemplate a past decision, I've found that applying the following process to past decisions that still bother you provides insights for future decision-making successes.

Effective Decision Definitions—A Short Course

What is the use of running when we are not on the right road?
German proverb

If you want to reach clarity on your decisions faster and easier, make it a routine to define them. The structure will automatically provide the pattern for the action that follows. This and the following chapter give you ammunition to identify relevant elements of your decision and put them together into "a one-pager." It is based on observed issues with decision definitions in my work with decision makers; it lists common traps and ways to avoid them. It is a simple but effective process. After you do it a couple of times, you can define your decisions in 15 minutes or less.

The characteristic feature of this process of defining decisions is its focus on concerns related to the decision. It also clarifies the decision objective versus the decision question and formulates the decision in a constructive, positive way that is conducive to overcoming concerns and arriving at a clear choice.

PART **II**

Definitions

A decision is defined when the Decision Objective and Decision Constraints are identified.

Decision Definition = Objective + Constraints

Decision Map = Decision Definition + Solution Options

The main, standard components of a decision map are represented graphically in Figure 6-1.

Decision Map

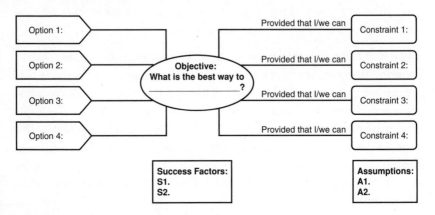

FIGURE 6-1
Standard Components of a Decision Map

Key Point

**The clearer you are on the decision definition,
the sharper your aim.
The sharper your aim, the more varied and
targeted your options become.
The better your options, the more likely you are
to hit the target.**

Note that links between the objective and constraints carry meaning. The objective and constraints are combined into one decision definition statement with the phrase "provided that I/we can" connecting constraints to the main objective. For example, a decision definition can read as follows:

> Objective: "What is the best way to cut costs *provided that we can*
>
> Constraint 1: Retain employees and
>
> Constraint 2: Improve process efficiency?"

The following discussion on clarifying the main objective, constraints, and decision options will help you put your decision map together.

The process of creating a decision map can be incredibly beneficial in focusing the decision on the fundamental purpose behind it, in understanding main concerns related to it, and in clarifying the decision overall. The whole decision might become clear as a result of this process, as was demonstrated by several decision makers who made their decisions at the completion of the decision map.

However, I have to stress that a decision map is a creation of the rational mind. Even though the main parts of a decision are identified, there might be other issues involved in the decision that are not captured in the decision map. I have seen decision makers come up with additional constraints and define additional options while they were contemplating their decision in the Clarity State. Moreover, I have seen executives change their perspective on the issue, in which case the prior decision map became invalid. It is important to realize that the creation of a decision map is only one part of the Clarity State Decision-Making technique—it's very powerful, but it's just one step in making the right decision.

Clarity of Objective

> *What is conceived well is expressed clearly.*
> Nicolas Boileau[3]

Effective executives set broad, overarching objectives and lead their teams to achieve them. However, we all frequently fall into common traps in defining objectives, especially under time pressure. Even experienced decision makers are not immune. The following are the five most common traps that you should avoid when setting your objective.

Trap #1: Formulating the Objective as an Option Selection

Many people confuse the decision question ("What should I do in this situation—choose alternative 1 or 2?") with the decision objective ("What do I want to achieve by making this decision?").

Key Point
The decision objective is *not* the decision question!

This seems like an obvious fact. Yet many decision makers formulate their objectives in terms of options selection. But when asked "What are you trying to achieve? What's the objective?" many decision makers, especially in smaller companies, paused in a startled manner and only then started really focusing on the objective behind their decision. In many cases, this was the first time they had asked themselves this question since they had started wrestling with the decision.

The decision question is usually obvious to a decision maker. Selecting the right objective, however, is more of an art than a science, because many objectives, evaluation parameters, concerns, and issues are usually present in each decision[4,5]. Consider the case of David, who is working on his decision objective.

EXAMPLE 6-3: DAVID—SHOULD I STAY OR SHOULD I LEAVE?

David is a founder and CEO of a company that has grown successfully. The company is in the process of acquiring another business. The acquisition target is of a similar size, and the deal will be more of a merger of equals than an acquisition. The deal requires David to vacate the top slot and become president of the company, reporting to the person who currently runs the other business. As the deal is being structured, David is faced with a decision: "Should I stay or should I leave?" He realizes that a new management team will need to be put in place, and the merged company will not be the same type of company that he came to love working for. He also knows that his expertise is needed in the business—it is less critical than it used to be, but it is still extremely important.

Obviously, this is one of those decisions that have layers of history and thus complexity within them, involving not only business needs but personal issues as well. What is David's objective in making this decision?

As you can see, the decision question is different from the decision objective. The decision question is clear: "What should I do? Should I leave or stay?" The decision objective may be one of the following: "Find ways to integrate the companies faster (something that I can impact directly), so that my financial return is increased before I leave," or "Find the best way to operate in the environment most productive for me." One of the main challenges for David in the formulation of his decision definition will be to select an objective that will be congruent with his personal desires and business needs.

Lesson #1   It is critical that you become clear on both the decision question and the decision objective!

> **Exercise**
>
> Write down the decision question and the decision objective for the decision you selected in Chapter 1. Use the worksheet at the end of this chapter as you work with your decision through the exercises.

Trap #2: Incorporating Too Many Parameters into the Objective

Each decision has a number of objectives, concerns, and evaluation parameters. However, if you put all these parameters into the objective, you will diffuse the decision's aim and limit the number of alternative solutions.

Consider Jim's situation.

> ### EXAMPLE 6-4: JIM—PRICE INCREASE
>
> Jim is the CEO of a manufacturing company with over $500 million in revenue. His company serves a diverse set of industries with products that are based on two technologies. In several industry segments, the revenue is spread in an uneven manner—with 80 percent coming from several large customers and the rest from a large number of much smaller customers.
>
> Jim's team is having a problem with one of these customers, a Fortune 100 company that commands the revenue flow in one of the industry segments. Jim asked a team to investigate the reasons why the overall margin from the business with this customer is close to zero. After much detailed analysis, the team came to the conclusion that there are several unprofitable products in the

portfolio of products that the company supplies to this customer. Jim is faced with the decision question: "What should be done?"

Jim's company has a long history with this customer: reengineering manufacturing processes to deliver more cost-effective products, providing just-in-time delivery, and designing many custom products for this customer. Some of the products in the portfolio are unique, and some can be obtained from competition at the same or lower price. Jim and the team are concerned that if they approach this customer with a price increase proposal, they will lose revenue in the long run.

At least three major issues can be incorporated into the objective: a) not losing revenue from this customer over the short and long term, b) improving profitability and taking it to a certain level, and c) having a good relationship with this customer. What is Jim's objective?

Suppose Jim defines the objective by incorporating all of these parameters: "Retain revenue level, improve profitability, and retain a good relationship with this customer." In this formulation, his main aim is unclear. Is he primarily after profitability and willing to have less revenue from this customer long-term, but profitable revenue only? Or is his intent to have a relationship with this customer even at a loss because such a relationship serves as a prominent case study? The solutions will be different depending on how he chooses the main objective.

Lesson #2   **Separate your objective from concerns and other parameters involved in the decision. For clarity, focus the main objective on *one* parameter.**

I am not suggesting discarding the other important parameters involved in the decision. We will incorporate them into your decision definition as constraints. You will gain significant additional flexibility in the breadth and depth of solution options by having these parameters participate in the decision definition as constraints rather than as a part of the main objective, as we will discuss later in the book. As you work on finding and formulating your main objective, keep a separate list with other objectives involved in the decision.

It is also important to notice concerns related to the decision and keep track of them. For example, the fact that David will have to vacate the top slot is a concern for him—he does not like stepping down. He is worried about other people's reactions and his position in the world. After thinking about it, he decides that "having the top spot" is definitely not his main objective, but it's an important concern that might have a bearing on his decision. Keep track of such concerns in a separate list as you formulate your main objective.

Trap #3: Making the Objective Too Narrow

The objective should be broad enough not to limit your options. In Jim's case, if he positions his objective too narrowly ("Address a margin situation in this customer's portfolio"), he might be faced with the unpleasant task of approaching this customer with a price increase. If he thinks about it more broadly ("Find ways to bring this customer's business to x% profitability"), more options will be open to him—expand this customer's business with unique products *and* resolve the current profitability issue.

You also need to find the fundamental reason for this decision, the one that is tied to the vision of your business.

> **Lesson #3   Look for a broad or meta-level objective that is fundamental to the vision of your business.**

Here is one way to do it. You can find the main, fundamental objective by starting with a decision question and asking "Why is this important?" When you have an answer, ask again until you find the objective that represents the main reason why you are interested in this decision.

In the previous example of Jim's decision, Jim's question is "What should be done in relation to this customer's portfolio?"

Why is this important? Because he wants to "Address the margin situation in this customer's portfolio."

Why? Because he wants to "Make this customer's business profitable." Moreover, he wants to "Find ways to bring this customer's business to x% profitability."

Why? Because Jim intends to run an increasingly profitable company. Therefore, a broader objective can be "Increase the company's overall profitability."

> ### Exercise
>
> Taking into account lessons learned previously in this chapter, clarify your decision objective. Make sure that it is focused on one parameter and is tied to the vision of your business.

Trap #4: Allowing a Personal Objective to Take a Backseat

We often disregard our personal objectives in our decisions. Frequently, personal and business issues conflict or become so tightly intertwined that it is difficult to separate them. Mature executives rarely allow this to happen. David's situation, described previously, is a good example of personal and business objectives intertwined. In the search for a main objective, it is important to clearly identify personal and business objectives separately.

In David's case, he has a sense that he will not like the change in the company's environment after the acquisition. His personal objective may be to "work in a friendly environment." His business objective may be "Make sure that the company integrates the acquisition successfully," or, taking performance to a higher level, "Accelerate the company's growth by leveraging this acquisition." In this formulation, his personal and business objectives are not congruent. If he stays, he will add value to the effort of the integration of the two companies, but it's likely that he will not like the environment in which he will be working. In this situation, one objective should take precedence and be named the main decision objective, and the other should be added to the concern list.

Luckily for David, there is a way to make his personal and business objectives congruent. As he thinks about the financial side of the transaction, he sees more and more incentives to stay rather than leave.

David has a sizeable share of the company's stock. He believes that after the acquisition, especially if the integration is done properly, the combined company has a real shot at going public within a short period of time. However, if he leaves, he would not be able to impact the integration and the size of his financial return as a result. This contemplation makes David decide on his main objective—"Increase my financial return," an objective that is congruent with the business objective of "Integrate the two companies successfully."

Lesson #4   Clearly identify personal and business objectives. Look for ways to make them congruent.

Most often, business and personal objectives can be made congruent. In rare cases when you cannot find a way to make them congruent, pick either a personal or a business goal that should be the main objective for this decision. Sometimes, such a selection is easier said than done. I've encountered several cases when this choice had to be made with the help of the Clarity State.

Add the other objective to the concern list. In David's case, the concern about the change in the company's environment has not gone away; it should be added as a concern to the decision definition. However, it is not the main objective of David's decision.

Trap #5: Formulating the Objective in a Sloppy Way with Unclear Metrics

Words are very important in formulating your decision objective. Consider the objective "High return to shareholders." What does this mean? Does your company want to *deliver* high return to shareholders *continuously*? Or at some point *produce* a high return? What is *high*? Does it mean that you are not delivering a good return now?

I've found that starting the formulation of the objective with "What is the best way to" is especially effective. Formulated in this manner, your mind is looking for not just some option to satisfy the objective, but for the best way to do so. It also makes the objective *actionable* by necessitating a verb, such as "What is the best way to *achieve, develop, gain, leverage…*"

After you zero in on one parameter that is the most important issue in this decision and tie it to the vision of your business, the main objective will be at a high, conceptual level. In order for the objective to make sense in the current situation, you need to ground it in the specific issues with which you are wrestling. The way to do this is to combine the high-level objective with the decision question.

For example, in Jim's case, his objective may read as follows: "What is the best way to increase the company's profitability level and address the current customer situation?" Or, formulated with a specific metric in mind, "What is the best way to bring this customer's business to x% profitability level?"

In David's case, his main objective reads as follows: "What is the best way to create an environment so that I can increase my financial return over the next 18 months?"

Lesson #5a   Formulate your objective in an actionable way that includes an action verb in the formulation, such as, "What is the best way to *achieve, develop, gain, leverage...*"

Exercise

Probe into the personal motives related to your decision. Are they congruent with the business objectives? Also, make sure that your decision objective is formulated in an actionable way that is integrated with the decision question.

Now that you have developed an objective that is connected to the high-level goals of your business or your personal goals and have grounded it with the specifics of the current environment, the last critical step is to identify ways in which you would measure the achievement of this objective.

Think of several metrics that would measure the realization of your objective. The more, the better. You need a way to evaluate the results so that the result satisfies your objective. This process will make the objective real in your mind.

Whenever one analyzes the way a truly effective, a truly right, decision has been reached, one finds that a great deal of work and thought went into finding the appropriate measurement.
Peter Drucker[6]

Lesson #5b   Identify clear success factors related to your main objective.

> **Exercise**
>
> How would you measure whether your decision was a success? What evidence procedure will demonstrate to you that the decision achieved its purpose? Who will be able to attest to this success? Is it you or other people? How would they measure the success of your undertaking? Is their measurement different from yours? If so, how?

In Jim's case, the success metric is clear—x% profitability in business with this customer. In David's case, it is less clear. What level of financial return is he looking for? What is his base level—the return he would have received without staying to integrate the acquisition? What is the level of increase in financial return from this activity? When these questions are answered clearly, his aim is clear and precise.

The following simple process summarizes ways to avoid the previous traps and make your decision focus clear.

Process for Clarifying a Decision Objective

- Start with the decision question.
- Ask "Why is this important?" several times until you get to a fundamental reason behind this decision that is connected to the vision of the business.
- Focus on *one* parameter in your objective.
- Incorporate the decision question into the objective. Formulate the objective starting with "What is the best way to…"
- Identify success metrics.

A well-formulated, clear objective can serve as a major step in making a smart decision. In Jim's case, because his decision is driven by a well-formulated, clear objective, his company is likely to develop a creative way to work with this customer by reworking the product portfolio for a win-win that will benefit the customer and the company. In David's case, in an effort to satisfy the objective, he is likely to develop a plan for how his skills can most effectively benefit the integration of an acquired business.

Worksheet 6-1: Clarifying a Decision Objective

Decision question: _____

    Why is this important? _____

    Why is this important? _____

    (Continue asking this question until you get to the main reason you are interested in this decision.)

Main objective connected to the vision of your business:

_____

Main objective with a decision question incorporated into it:

What is the best way to

_____?

Success metrics:

1. _____

2. _____

3. _____

Other objectives:

1. _____

2. _____

3. _____

Relevant concerns:

1. _____

2. _____

3. _____

CHAPTER 7

Escaping Handcuffs— How to Achieve Clarity of Constraints

Order and simplification are the first steps towards the mastery of a subject—the actual enemy is the unknown.
Thomas Mann[1]

A good objective gives your decision a clear aim. The purpose of constraints is to further sharpen this aim with other important relevant factors.

What Is a Constraint?

> **Definition**
>
> A **constraint** is
> a condition that a decision maker wants a selected solution to address
> and/or
> a parameter by which solutions will be evaluated
> and/or
> an additional objective behind the decision

By their nature, constraints limit the scope of the applicable solutions. If you miss some important issues in the definition of your decision—taking into account a clear risk, for example—you'll have more solutions to consider. As a result, your decision-making will be easier, but with questionable success. If you load your objective with irrelevant issues (which I call false constraints), your decision-making will be easier, because you will have only a couple of options to consider, but you are likely to select a faulty path.

In over a quarter of cases, decision makers that I interviewed had issues with missing or false constraints. Identifying a missing constraint or removing a false one from consideration makes a decision clearer.

Key Point
Identifying and defining relevant constraints is a major step toward making a clear decision.

Defining clear constraints is an issue with decision makers in small *and* large companies. Data from interviews suggests that, as a matter of routine, small company executives do not clearly define objectives, not to mention constraints. Decision makers in large companies, due to a better-developed decision support infrastructure, usually have a main objective clearly formulated by the team designated to propose a solution to a particular business issue. However, this does not necessarily apply to constraints. The team might be unaware of other efforts in the company, for example, or a strategic direction that a CEO wants to implement in the future that can have a bearing on the decision. Thus, constraints usually are not clearly defined.

Exercise
Using the definitions presented previously, identify constraints relevant to the decision you are working with.

Typically, decision makers include only one or two obvious sub-objectives as constraints in their decision definition. These sub-objectives are usually the result of the process of clarifying the decision objective. *Deeper issues get missed.* Knowing how to identify and properly define constraints can be a major stumbling block to clarity.

Key Point

Effective executives know that the most important decision constraints come from areas of concern, risk, difficulty, or disagreement related to a decision in addition to subobjectives.

Consider Brenda's example.

EXAMPLE 7-1: BRENDA—SIX SIGMA QUALITY INITIATIVE

Brenda is the CEO of an insurance company that has started losing customers. Her company is considering a Six Sigma quality initiative.

Here's Brenda's formulation of the decision definition: "What is the best way to achieve higher growth through using quality processes as a competitive weapon (main objective), provided that we can quickly reverse customer attrition (Constraint 1)?"

Brenda could list only one constraint that was a clear subobjective for the decision. Her feeling was that she was missing something, but she was not sure what that was.

The following are five common traps that you should avoid in identifying and defining your decision constraints.

Traps to Avoid

Trap #1: Excluding Concerns as Factors Relevant to a Decision

In our discussion with Brenda after she developed the decision definition presented in Example 7-1, a number of issues came out.

Brenda is new to the company. She is concerned about how people will react to the sweeping quality effort. Her company does not have well documented processes or clear metrics, especially in the area of working with customers. She is concerned that an effort to force metrics on everyone from the top down could come as a big culture shock and thus fail in the long run.

She is also concerned about the availability of managers who can lead and execute this initiative. She knows how much effort this initiative can consume, having worked for a company with a well-developed quality effort. She realizes that a whole new organization will need to be built in order to make it happen.

I asked Brenda to write down her concerns. Here is her list:

a. I am concerned about the acceptance of the proposed initiative by the company.

b. I am worried about the push-back related to metrics.

c. I am not sure that we can execute. How long would it take us to put together an organization that will drive this effort?

These types of concerns make a decision difficult. More importantly, if not addressed in the eventual solution, they can serve as barriers to a successful implementation.

Lesson #1   Focus on concerns related to your decision! Concerns qualify as constraints. A good decision has to address them!

Asking yourself the simple question "Why is this decision difficult for me?" will identify some of the concerns you should take into account.

> **Exercise**
>
> List easily identifiable concerns related to your decision—the ones that you can quickly name. Use Worksheet 7-1, shown later in this chapter, to keep track of them.

Trap #2: Formulating Constraints in Negative Terms

You might have noticed a general principle that when you focus on something negative in your thoughts, the amount of negative feedback from your environment increases. As a result, your thoughts may become even more negative, and you are quickly on a downward slope to a much more negative experience. The negative issue can be related to your or someone else's behavior, or something in your environment or your job, for example.

It's the same with constraints. Negative formulation tends to get your mind thinking in the same negative way. By their nature, concerns are formulated negatively. Reformulating them in a positive way *shifts your mind into a constructive and creative mode* of searching for a solution to address these constraints.

> **Lesson #2** **Formulate constraints as objectives to overcome the concerns they are based on. Make sure that you use an action verb in defining an objective, such as *satisfy, improve, address, generate,* or *enable*.**

Let's use Brenda's concerns to demonstrate this conversion. The first two concerns are similar, so Brenda combined them into one concern. Here is her resulting concern list:

a. I am concerned about the acceptance of the proposed quality initiative by the company, especially metrics.

b. I am not sure that we can execute. How long would it take us to put together an organization that will drive this effort?

She converts the first concern into the following constraint:

Constraint based on Concern a: Gain acceptance of the proposed quality initiative by major stakeholders in the company, especially metrics.

Similarly, she converts the second concern into a constructive constraint or subobjective:

Constraint based on Concern b: Build the team to execute.

Here is Brenda's resulting decision definition incorporating the objective, the obvious subobjective that she identified initially, and newly identified constraints. A graphical representation is shown in Figure 7-1.

"Objective: What is the best way to achieve higher growth through using quality processes as a competitive weapon

provided that we can

-   Constraint 1: Quickly reverse customer attrition (initial subobjective)

-   Constraint 2: Gain acceptance for the effort, especially metrics, by major stakeholders in the company (based on Concern a) and

-   Constraint 3: Build a team to execute (based on Concern b)"?

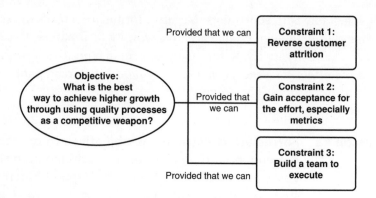

FIGURE 7-1
Brenda's Decision Definition

Trap #3: Missing Important Parameters as Part of a Decision

If these parameters are so important, why do we routinely miss them? It is because they are built into our environment or personal style to such an extent that we do not notice them. Usually, these concerns are vague and manifest themselves as uneasiness about the decision. They frequently surface in a discussion about the decision, generally as a result of direct questions by a third party probing specific areas of concern.

The following are several areas of concern that we commonly overlook. During interviews, I routinely asked decision makers to consider the following specific areas with an objective to identify missing issues related to the decision.

Commonly Overlooked Area of Concern: Corporate Culture

In their seminal work *Decision Making at the Top: The Shaping of Strategic Direction*[2], Gordon Donaldson and Jay Lorsch examined the process of how companies arrive at their goals. They worked with 12 companies that were major forces in their respective industries at that time. They found that each firm had a set of unique beliefs, or corporate culture, usually based on the founders' beliefs, which influenced decision-making in the company. These beliefs drastically impact the establishment of internal management systems, goals, and means to achieve them.

Donaldson and Lorsch noted that

- A company's historical belief system, or culture, acts as a powerful constraint on every decision.
- Decision makers themselves have difficulty in identifying beliefs due to their personal adherence to these beliefs.

If such beliefs are not made explicit, they can serve as powerful barriers to new ideas—you are likely to stay "in the cultural box." Or, on the other side of the spectrum, your decision might conflict with these powerful beliefs. If you are unaware of this fact, your solution might not work within the current culture.

Notice that the first two concerns on Brenda's initial list are related to cultural issues.

> **Lesson #3   Make cultural beliefs relevant to your decision explicit in your decision definition, removing the potential for them to become barriers to new strategies and solutions. Identify cultural beliefs that conflict with your decision, and list them as concerns.**

Ed Schein in his book *The Corporate Culture Survival Guide*[3] recommends performing a "culture audit" in order for the company to be aware of its unwritten rules and take them into account in decision-making. However, this is not a common practice, especially in smaller companies.

Another way to better understand your company's corporate culture is to contemplate the following questions in the Clarity State that probe your company's beliefs about strategy-setting, risk, and self-sufficiency. Be creative; compare your decision to other areas of the company's innate beliefs.

a.   What habits does my company have for achieving objectives? Is my decision congruent with these means?

For example, if one of your company's beliefs is "innovate in bite sizes," and you are trying to develop a full line of new products that are intended to be disruptive in the market, you should be aware of this fact.

b. How does my company handle risk? Is the risk involved in my decision higher or lower than my company's risk tolerance level?

> For example, your company's belief may be "stick with major technological breakthroughs," and you are trying to be incremental and not technically innovative in your decision approach. Or, on the contrary, your decision recommends an action path with a higher degree of risk than your company normally accepts. As a result, your solution may not be appropriate in your company's culture.

c. What are the company's behaviors regarding how problems are handled? Is my decision congruent with them?

> For example, if your company believes "never buy market share" and you are including price decrease in your decision, beware.

Commonly Overlooked Area of Concern: Availability of People Critical to the Implementation of the Solution

To be fair, it's not the case that decision makers do not think about properly staffing new efforts. We do, but in our drive to move forward, we don't necessarily think about it in depth. We often assume that resources are available for the implementation.

In the course of my work with decision makers, there were several situations when leaders remembered encountering resistance from their teams in relation to a strategic initiative they were contemplating. The resistance, as it later turned out, was a team's way to communicate to the leader that they were "swamped" and could not successfully handle yet another cross-company effort at that time.

Another mistake is common in the current "stretched thin" corporate environment. A company sometimes assumes that a manager who has demonstrated great results in the past can be asked to lead the new effort without giving too much thought to the time needed in transition. The manager needs enough time to ensure that the prior effort he or she was managing continues to perform well.

Commonly Overlooked Area of Concern: Realism of the Proposed Solution

Obviously, assessing the company's ability to execute a proposed solution is a subjective matter, and at the end of the day, the leader's opinion is the decisive one. And, obviously, if you listen to naysayers too much, no "ahead of the pack" strategies would be ever executed. It is a delicate balance.

However, when red flags are raised, you should contemplate this area of concern in more depth. In his autobiography[4], Jack Welch recounts his decision to acquire Kidder Peabody, one of Wall Street's oldest investment banking firms, as the "worst nightmare" and "a terrible mistake." Three finance-savvy board members were against the acquisition. Welch thought about the raised concerns but was too focused on the benefits of the deal to really take the concerns into account. He decided to proceed and convinced the board to unanimously go his way. Subsequently discovered issues made the acquisition experience painful for Welch and GE.

Lesson #3a   **Check your decision against commonly overlooked areas of concern to identify missing factors.**

Exercise

Think about your company's culture and other factors surrounding your decision. Any concerns you might be missing? Identify additional concerns related to your decision, and add them to the concern list.

Trap #4: Ignoring Emotions and Attachments in Defining Decisions

We are sure to be losers when we quarrel with ourselves; it is a civil war, and in all such contentions, triumphs are defeats.
Charles Caleb Colton[5]

In my discussions with decision makers, there were a number of situations when a leader was rationally convinced about the rightness of a certain path but was reluctant to move forward. The gut was saying one thing, but the rational mind said another.

I strongly believe that such instinctive messages need to be listened to and made explicit as much as possible. I am not advocating taking action based totally on instinct, even though it does make sense in rare situations, but rather recognizing the internal resistance and taking time to uncover the reasons behind it.

It is rare when a decision needs to be made immediately. There is usually time to "soak on it," as Linn Draper, the former CEO of AEP, says—a practice that is now adopted by many of his current and former subordinates[6].

Lesson #4a   If you feel uneasy about a decision, spend time in detecting the cause. Identify and include the cause in your decision definition.

One way to gain clarity about an internal concern is to focus on this area of discomfort or fogginess to the exclusion of all other thoughts in the Clarity State. When you focus on this vagueness, putting words to it, trying out different thoughts about it, you will finally find a viewpoint that clicks. Once you find that viewpoint, you have clarity about the issue, and you resolve your internal conflict.

Our perception is also colored by what we expect to see (such influences are called cognitive factors) and what we want to see. Factors that deal with hopes, desires, and emotional attachments are known as "motivational" factors. These include our need to view ourselves in a positive manner, the tendency to view events in a way we would like to see them turn out, and the desire to avoid regret, among others.

Lesson #4b   Identify and include your motivations and expectations in your decision definition.

Ask yourself the following key questions in the Clarity State in order to discover cognitive and motivational factors:

a.   Am I motivated to see things in a certain way?

b.   What expectations do I bring into the situation?

c.   Am I afraid that I will regret having pushed myself to an unconventional solution?

People are known to distort their judgment to avoid regret. People experience greater regret when they choose an action that deviates from the norm and turns out poorly because they can easily imagine a much better outcome of a more conventional choice.

Emotions associated with the situation related to a decision can serve as good indicators of concerns present but not accounted for in a decision definition. We will discuss ways of identifying concerns behind emotions and incorporating them as constraints later in the book.

Disagreement within the team or with the board, for example, can make a decision difficult, as many decision makers commented during interviews. In cases when disagreement accompanies a decision, I've found it effective to incorporate these areas of disagreement as constraints into the decision definition. Taking these areas into account allows the whole team to focus on creative solutions, the process that eventually results in resolving the disagreement. More on this topic appears in Chapter 9, "Pick a Fight!—How to Get the Most Out of Clashing Opinions."

Lesson #4c   Identify and include concerns related to emotions and disagreements in the decision definition.

Exercise:

At this point, you should have filled the left side of Worksheet 7-1 with areas of concern, risk, and difficulty, as well as emotional, motivational, and other factors. Some of these issues may be repetitive. Select the most relevant ones.

Convert these concerns into constraints, as discussed earlier.

Trap #5: Incorporating Perceived Constraints into the Decision

Mike Armstrong, a former CEO of AT&T and Chairman of Comcast, shared with me that based on his years of decision-making and reflection on these decisions, one of the major traps in decision-making is wrong or biased assumptions. This is where perceived or false constraints typically come from.

"Never assume" is a well-known adage. The problem, of course, is that, like cultural beliefs, when you are under the spell of an assumption, you rarely know it[7]. The presence of this false assumption might be limiting your view and your options. Often, when you make an assumption explicit, you can develop a strategy that is creative and non-obvious, as the following example demonstrates.

EXAMPLE 7-2: CHRIS—A NEW MARKET STRATEGY

Chris is an SVP of Marketing for a beverage company. The company embarked on an aggressive entry into the South American market with a specialty drink. Its major competitor is strong in this particular market segment.

Chris is working on strategies to increase his company's product appeal with an objective to capture additional market share.

During the exercise of defining his decision, Chris realizes that he has been under the spell of a simple assumption. He assumed that the rival company would focus on this segment with more products and would be as strong as it always has been. The latest developments, however, were actually pointing to a different story. The competitor had shifted its main focus to a different market segment. It was working on an acquisition in that segment and had introduced at least three new products there.

Chris realized that his assumption about the rival's current focus and strength in his company's market segment was wrong. As a result, having made this assumption, he was leading his company in the wrong direction. He was focusing on incremental measures, such as increasing the existing products' appeal, rather than creating strategies for capturing the market lead while the competitor was distracted.

Experienced CEOs suggest building a routine of assumption checking into the decision-making process, especially when a critical business decision is involved. They suggest having discussions with team members or outsiders for the purpose of identifying assumptions and biases behind the decision.

Lesson #5 **List your and other people's assumptions related to the decision. Check them for validity in the current environment. Remove perceived constraints from your decision definition that are based on false assumptions.**

Clarity State is useful in identifying assumptions. Answer the following questions in the Clarity State that probe into the bases behind your decision.

a. Are you using any "rules of thumb" in your decision?

b. What major pieces of information are you using in this decision? How readily is this information available? How old is it?

c. What main facts (about the market, product, and so on) are you using in this decision? How old are these facts? Have they been checked recently?

d. Do you have a strong opinion about the situation related to your decision? What is it? What is it based on? Is it an assumption?

Be creative. You are checking your decision against common behaviors of overconfidence in judgment (failing to collect key factual information because you are too sure of your assumptions and opinions) and shortsighted shortcuts (relying inappropriately on "rules of thumb" such as implicitly trusting the most readily available information or anchoring too much on convenient facts).

PART II

Exercise

Using the process just described, identify major assumptions that you and other people are making about your decision. Make sure that you write them down—use Worksheet 7-1. For each assumption, list several reasons why it may be wrong. Do any of these reasons "ring true" to you? If so, probe deeper—you might be relying on a false assumption.

We will work further with the assumptions on your list in Chapter 11, "Becoming a Frame Artist—How to Master Clarity of Perspective."

In summary, the process of clarifying constraints consists of ways to identify them and then convert them into positive subobjectives to overcome concerns and disagreements, deal with risks, and address emotions.

Process for Clarifying Decision Constraints

The changing of a vague difficulty into a specific, concrete form is a very essential element of effective decision-making.

- Compile a list of concerns.
  - List easily identifiable concerns by asking "Why is this decision difficult for me?"
  - Review commonly overlooked areas of concern for missing factors.
  - Identify emotional, motivational, and other concerns.
- Convert each concern into an objective to overcome the concern.
- Make sure to use an action verb in defining an objective, such as *satisfy*, *improve*, *address*, *generate*, or *enable*.
- Tie decision constraints to the decision objective with "provided that I/we can..."
- Identify and remove perceived or false constraints.

Worksheet 7-1: Clarifying Decision Constraints

I. Easily identifiable concerns (I am concerned about...)   Objectives to overcome concerns

1. _____
2. _____
3. _____
4. _____

1. _____
2. _____
3. _____
4. _____

Use action verbs in converting concerns into objectives such as find, identify.

II. Concerns based on commonly missed parameters   Objectives to overcome concerns

1. _____
2. _____
3. _____
4. _____

1. _____
2. _____
3. _____
4. _____

Use action verbs in converting concerns into objectives such as satisfy, improve.

III. Concerns related to emotions, expectations, motivations   Objectives to overcome concerns

(I expect to...)
(I want to see...)
(I fear that...)

1. _____
2. _____
3. _____
4. _____

1. _____
2. _____
3. _____
4. _____

Use action verbs in converting concerns into objectives such as gain, enable.

IV. Assumptions   Is it a perceived constraint?

1. _____
2. _____
3. _____

1. _____
2. _____
3. _____

PART II

Example: Achieving Clarity of Decision Definition—Putting Together a Decision Map

Let's use the following example to demonstrate the process of putting together a decision map consisting of all the elements, objectives, constraints, and solution options.

EXAMPLE 7-3: LIN—ACHIEVING GROWTH THROUGH CUSTOMER INTEGRATION

Lin is the CEO of a company that is considering a total revamp of its IT system. Lin has a vision of the new IT system helping the business become integrated with customers, thus positioning the company above all competitors. Two people on his team disagree, both stating objections: one, the system is too expensive, and two, what if it does not work?

Both concerns are valid. How should Lin structure a decision definition to take them into account?

Lin works on creating the decision definition by following the rules for identifying the main objective. He starts with the decision question and asks himself "Why is it important?" until he gets to the fundamental reason behind his decision. His decision question is "What is the best IT system for us?" One of the reasons for doing this is to achieve tight integration with customer processes. He says, "It is important for us because we want to beat everyone else and be able to do it first— we'll get a great differentiation in the market! And this is exciting because we will be able to grow much faster than everyone else." Having gone through this reasoning, Lin decides that the fundamental reason behind his decision is the company's accelerated growth. He now combines this high-level objective with the decision question, and his objective is now clearly defined: "What is the best IT system to accelerate the business growth?"

This main objective has left out one major parameter by which Lin's company will evaluate the effectiveness of this new IT system— namely, the ability to integrate with customers. His team needs to make sure that the integration capabilities can differentiate the company in the marketplace. So, he adds this main parameter to the decision definition as a constraint or a subobjective: "Obtain differentiation through customer integration."

Lin has specific areas in mind for the customer integration, which he notes in the success factors:

1. Immediate visibility of the customer's shipping needs directly from the customer's systems.
2. All documentation handled electronically.
3. Ability for customers to easily adjust/schedule shipments online.
4. Online visibility of accurate, frequently updated (every half hour) schedules and committed deliveries open to customers and us.

Now he can work on the concerns raised by his team members. The first concern imposes a financial constraint on the objective, and the second forces the company to define the level of acceptable risk as a result of the IT system conversion. In this case, Lin's objective or vision of making his business grow through integration with customers can be made more feasible if Lin constrains it with these two concerns that limit financial risk and guard against unsuccessful implementation. Besides, by adding these two concerns to the decision definition, it gives him a way to help bring the two objecting team members to his side.

Step 2 of the process of clarifying constraints calls for formulating concerns into subobjectives that overcome these concerns by utilizing an action verb. For example, in Lin's situation, one concern is that the system is too expensive. A related objective to address this concern can be worded as "Minimize financial investment." The second constraint is "What if the new system doesn't work?" A related subobjective to address this concern can be worded as "Ensure successful implementation."

As Lin goes through assumption checking, he realizes that there are two underlying assumptions behind this decision that might be wrong. First, in his excitement about the vision, he is assuming that his company is the only one that is thinking about such customer integration. Wrong! In the current Internet proliferation, all competitors are thinking about it! Second, he is assuming that his company knows what "differentiation" means in the current environment. However, he might be too short-term in his approach, thinking of immediate capabilities that can be provided but not thinking enough of differentiators for the future.

This realization makes Lin add another constraint to the decision definition: "Deliver the first capabilities in three months." He also decides to get a team to focus on brainstorming and clarifying the definition of customer integration differentiation.

So, here is Lin's decision definition:
"Objective: What is the best IT system to accelerate business growth, *provided that we can*

Constraint 1.   Obtain differentiation through customer integration

Constraint 2.   Minimize financial investment

Constraint 3.   Ensure successful implementation

Constraint 4.   Deliver the first capabilities in three months?"

A good test of whether a decision definition captures your intent in making this decision is to ask yourself: "If I select a solution that addresses all these parameters (the objective and constraints), will I be satisfied and happy with my decision?" If the answer is yes, you have created a good decision definition. In Lin's case, he decided that he would be satisfied if his team found an IT system that allowed tight customer integration, came within the set budget, and was installed successfully and quickly in the business. Obviously, this is a lot to ask, but he was confident in his team's ability to deliver.

Represented graphically, Lin's decision definition appears in Figure 7-2.

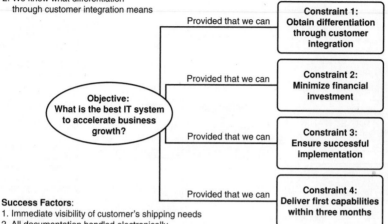

Assumptions:
1. We are unique in this approach
2. We know what differentiation through customer integration means

Provided that we can → **Constraint 1:** Obtain differentiation through customer integration

Provided that we can → **Constraint 2:** Minimize financial investment

Objective: What is the best IT system to accelerate business growth?

Provided that we can → **Constraint 3:** Ensure successful implementation

Provided that we can → **Constraint 4:** Deliver first capabilities within three months

Success Factors:
1. Immediate visibility of customer's shipping needs
2. All documentation handled electronically
3. Ability to easily adjust/schedule shipments online
4. Visibility of schedules and committed deliveries

FIGURE 7-2

Lin's Decision Definition

Now, in order to complete the decision map for Lin's decision, let's add solution options to the same chart.

His team is considering three solution options for an IT system:

1. Buy a new system from Vendor 1. The considered system has good customer integration functionality. The drawback of this system, however, is that it does not support some important business functions that are currently supported by the homegrown IT system.

2. Upgrade the current IT system. It was developed in-house 10 years ago. The technology is outdated, and the system does not support the envisioned customer integration functions. However, the system works very well for all other aspects of the business. Hence, it is possible to put together a technical team and add the needed functionality to the current system.

3. Bring in an IT system from a sister company. Lin's company belongs to a conglomerate consisting of seven businesses, distinctly different from each other. The team believes that an IT system from one of the sister companies might work for their business due to the fact that the business models are similar. However, the team needs to "dig" into the details before confirming this hypothesis.

Figure 7-3 shows a complete decision map of Lin's decision.

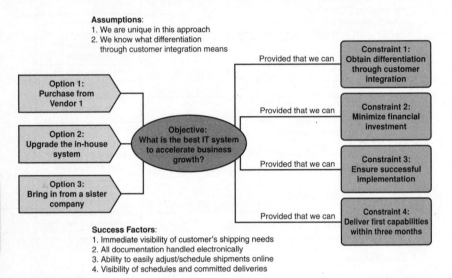

FIGURE 7-3
Lin's Decision Map

Exercise

Complete a decision map for your decision. If your current options do not address the objective and constraints, work through the best practices in the next section to expand solution options.

Expanding Solution Options

The solution is always simple—after you know what it is.
Anonymous

In working with decision makers on their current decisions, they usually did not have a problem identifying solution options related to a decision. However, I encountered several cases where solution options were limited and none of them could satisfy the stated objectives and constraints.

It was also the case that many decision makers developed new options, often by combining existing ones, while contemplating the decision in the Clarity State.

Key Point
It is a good practice to challenge solution options while completing the decision map.

The following is a list of best practices that can help you expand your list of solutions. It is based on advice from negotiation experts who are skilled at developing creative solution options and input from experienced decision makers.

Practice #1: Use One Good Option to Generate Others

The process is simple. Usually, an option has a feature that makes it good. However, that solution might not satisfy other parameters. Focus on the good feature and generalize it into an approach behind this feature. Think about other options that are the application of the same general approach to your problem.

For example, Option 1 in Lin's earlier example is to purchase an IT system from Vendor 1. The good feature of this solution is that the system has good customer integration functionality. However, it does not support other parts of the business as well as the existing system does. Going with this option will address the current need for customer integration capabilities but might jeopardize support for other parts of the business—a dangerous route. One generalization that can be developed from focusing on the good feature of this option is to look for systems that will *only* support the customer integration needs. This approach will result in an additional option of "Purchase only modules supporting customer integration capabilities that can be added to the existing system."

Practice #2: Look Through the Eyes of Experts

Another method of generating additional options is to look at the situation through the eyes of experts. For example, if you are faced with Lin's problem described previously, invent options for a technical person who will be involved in the installation of the new system, an outside consultant, a CFO, various internal users, a market analyst, a logistics expert, and so on.

PART II

It is also useful to look at the process of problem definition and analysis through the eyes of an expert rather than just generating solutions options. In this case, imagine that you are a certain type of expert, and go through the following steps:

1. **Define the problem**—What's wrong? What are the current symptoms? What are the "dislike" factors, contrasted with a preferred situation?

2. **Analysis**—Diagnose the problem, sort symptoms into categories that suggest causes of the problem, observe what is lacking, and note barriers to resolving the problem.

3. **Approaches**—What are possible strategies, prescriptions, or theoretical cures to address this problem? Generate broad ideas about what can be done.

4. **Action ideas**—What might be done? What specific action can be taken to deal with the problem?

Practice #3: Shuttle from Specific to General

A decision map is a representation of a decision at a certain level of detail chosen by the decision maker. Sometimes, this level of detail is inadequate for developing the right solution; it's either too high or too low. Going deeper into the details of one particular aspect of the decision (one of the constraints, for example) may generate more options.

In Lin's decision, if he needed more options about ensuring successful implementation, he could build a decision map focused on this subobjective, generate options satisfying that subobjective, and then raise these options to the level of the decision that we have defined in this chapter. This technique of decision layering is discussed in detail in Appendix B, "Additional Tips on Reducing Decision Complexity."

Practice #4: Vary the Strength of the Options

This is an exercise to invent stronger or weaker versions of existing options along parameters relevant to the decision. Even though it is a good exercise at the time of the decision map creation, it is more effective when done from the perspective of satisfying constraints, as discussed in Chapter 11.

Practice #5: Change the Scope of the Option

In this exercise, you consider varying not only the strength of the solutions but also their scope. For example, you can break your problem into smaller and more manageable units. Solutions may be partial, may apply to only certain geographic areas, or may remain in effect for only a limited period of time.

CHAPTER 8

Balancing Mind and Body—How to Learn from Your Emotional Cues

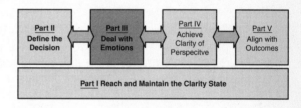

The heart has such an influence over the understanding that it is worthwhile to engage it in our interest.

Lord Chesterfield[1]

Emotions present a major difficulty in decision-making, which is complicated by the fact that limited information is available about how to deal with them in this context. However, even acknowledging the fact that emotions play a major part in decision-making is taboo in our macho business culture. We picture a great leader as a person who can "stay cool," reason under pressure, and make brilliant decisions that turn out great no matter what.

Two false beliefs govern our typical perspective on emotions in decision-making:

False Belief 1: You can separate from your emotions and stay "cool" when considering a decision or exercising a judgment.

It is also common to think that if emotions are present in decision-making, bad things happen. Most people believe that when we make bad decisions, they are based on emotion, but when we arrive at good decisions, they are based solely on reason[2].

False Belief 2: Emotions have a negative influence on decisions.

As a result, in the rare situation where emotions are present in decisions, our culture's picture-perfect business leader knows how to deal with them and does it perfectly every time.

But, in fact, what do we really know about the link between emotions and reason? Do emotions drive reason? And, if so, does this mean that we should separate from emotions before making a decision (a popular belief)? Or, does reason drive emotions? Or are they interdependent?

Recent Scientific Findings About the Link Between Emotions and Reason

It is part of our pedagogy to teach the operation of thinking, feeling and willing so that they may be made conscious. For if we do not know the difference between an emotion and a thought, we will know very little... We need to understand the components [of emotions] at work... in order to free their hold.

Mary Caroline Richards[3]

Neuroscientists have traced and documented the interdependencies between cognitive and emotional processes[4,5] and believe that these processes are tightly interrelated: "Emotions and cognition are best thought of as separate but interacting mental functions mediated by separate but interacting brain systems[4]." In addition, "...there is no way to separate them [emotions and reason][5]."

In common terms, emotions are present in everything we do[6]. Observations of the structure of the human brain show us that emotions are present in every decision we make. This finding flies in the face of the common belief (False Belief 1) in the advantage of "cool" over impassioned reasoning.

Key Point
Emotions are present in every decision we make; we cannot '"separate" from them. We have to learn to deal with emotions and take them into account in our actions.

It is interesting to note that only *30 percent* of the decision makers I interviewed admitted having emotions involved in their decisions. Such a low percentage might be the effect of False Belief 1—a good executive uses reasoning and not emotions to arrive at decisions—or just insensitivity to the present emotions. It is also interesting to note that *virtually all* decision makers discovered an emotion associated with the decision when they contemplated their decision in the Clarity State and were asked to do it. The emotion is always there, of course; we usually just do not pay attention to it.

Key Point
Clarity State enables the discovery of subtle emotions related to a situation.

Even though the interdependence between reason and emotion has been established, the question of cause and effect between emotion and reason has not yet been settled by science. Does cognition drive emotions, or do emotions drive cognition? There are theories supporting both.

One group of neuroscientists argues that cognition comes before the emotion. A person "appraises" the situation, and emotions follow. The authors of *Passion and Reason: Making Sense of Our Emotions*[2] state: "Our position is that emotion depends on reason, and that there is no way to separate them. To do so fails to recognize the role of reason in the arousal of emotions."

Neuroscientist Josef LeDoux[4] belongs to a group with an opposite opinion. He argues that emotional arousal dominates and controls thinking. It happens because, in his judgment, the center responsible for emotional responses (amygdala) has a greater influence on the center responsible for logic and reasoning (cortex) than the cortex has on the amygdala.

Now, what about whether the impact of emotions on decisions is good or bad? What about the common opinion that when we make bad decisions, they are based on emotions, and that when we make good decisions, they are based on reason, as represented by False Belief 2?

Scientists have studied the impact of positive and negative emotions on decision-making and have discovered interesting trends. In one study[7], decision makers in a positive mood, compared to the negative-mood participants, were more likely to interpret the strategic issue as an opportunity and displayed lower levels of risk-taking. The second study[7] replicated and extended the results of the first. Namely, if the issue was presented to participants in a framed form (as a threat or an opportunity), decision makers in a positive mood (called positive-effect participants) were more likely to disregard the frame and reframe the issue to their liking than were the decision makers in the negative mood (called negative-effect participants).

Another study[8] investigated the influence of positive-effect on clinical reasoning among practicing physicians using a simulated patient protocol. Physicians were asked to diagnose a case. Physicians in a good mood (in whom positive-effect had been induced) integrated information 19 percent earlier than control groups. They considered the diagnosis of liver disease, which was the correct diagnosis, and demonstrated less anchoring—distortion or inflexibility in thinking. Physicians' reasoning was examined for flawed processing, such as jumping to conclusions without sufficient evidence, and no abnormalities were detected.

These studies suggest that being in a positive mood while making a decision can have a positive impact on the decision itself.

Key Point

A decision maker in a positive mood is more likely to consider the problem as an opportunity, be able to overcome the limitations of a frame, find additional options, and arrive at a decision faster. Positive emotions have a positive impact on decisions.

Clarity State takes this finding into account—it is a highly positive emotional state. The results confirm the finding, as the following example demonstrates.

EXAMPLE 8-1: ANN—DEFINING A NEW STRATEGIC DIRECTION

Ann is a world-renowned marketing expert (and author of a number of books) who speaks on the subject frequently and runs a very successful company that she started 14 years ago. The company has shifted its direction a number of times, and Ann believes that the market demands another shift. She and her staff have been developing various options for a number of weeks. She is at the point of a decision.

Ann's main difficulty is selecting a strategy that takes into account her own personal desires. Personally, she likes to "push the envelope" and do something challenging and new. However, from a business standpoint, she knows that there are a number of very good options on the table that utilize proven-by-the-company approaches and that are moneymakers. It's unreasonable to give them up and focus on new, unproven services, but those new services are exactly the ones Ann gets excited about.

Ann decides to take a totally new positioning for the company and to provide certain services that have been proven to be effective for customers and that serve as moneymakers.

PART III

Her comment: "When you were explaining the Clarity State with its premise of being in a positive state of mind, I saw a bird in the window take off. Later, as I was contemplating my decision, I noticed that I feel bored and frustrated as I think about proven services. You asked me to find a positive point of view. I suddenly decided to ask myself, 'What are the things that will make me soar, like that bird in the window?' And the decision became absolutely clear at that point! It was unmistakable—I got this feeling of 'Let's go!', very excited and ready to execute."

In summary, our culture-based beliefs about emotions in decision-making turn out to be wrong according to recent scientific findings.

And yet, as a culture, we are profoundly under their spell, in operating companies and in educating business managers of the future. Obviously, it will take time before these new findings percolate into the culture and these beliefs start changing.

Learn from Your Emotions

The principle that emerges is that we should acknowledge that our emotions are part of our intuitive apparatus and treat them as data. It means listening to our emotions, getting in touch with them, being aware of what we are feeling—because those feelings provide information that must be taken into account, even when they are vague and we are not completely certain what we are feeling.
Robin Hogarth[9]

Emotions are there in every situation for a reason—they are trying to tell us something. The harder the situation, the more intense the emotions become. If we do not listen, we miss important, sometimes critical input that can help us resolve the situation.

The approach presented here uses emotions as tools to get to clarity in tough situations. It is based on several observations and lessons learned from working with executives on their current decisions.

Acknowledge Your Emotions

Observation #1: Acknowledging emotions that are related to the situation involved in the decision can be instructive to the decision maker and can quickly indicate the right decision.

The emotion may be subtle and vague, and it may take time to discover it. However, when decision makers do find and acknowledge the overriding emotion associated with the decision and work with it, in all cases this recognition served as a critical stepping-stone to making a clear decision.

As we've mentioned before, Clarity State is instrumental in finding subtle emotions. It is interesting to note that discovering an emotion was a surprise to many decision makers, as you can see from the following example.

EXAMPLE 8-2: TIM—PERSONNEL DECISION

Tim runs a $100 million medical services company that he founded along with another partner, Jon. Just a couple of months ago, Jon had a heart attack, and Tim had to take on all of his operational responsibilities in addition to his own. Tim is getting more and more uncomfortable with Richard, the company's COO/CFO, who previously reported to Jon. Tim sees that "things are falling through the cracks" when Richard manages them. The company is at a stage of new growth, expanding and opening operations in other states, and needs to raise expansion money. Richard, of course, can be very instrumental in leading the money-raising effort. Tim's decision question is "What to do about Richard?"

One of Tim's difficulties is that Jon has a better relationship with Richard and may object to any negative action related to him. The other problem is that if Tim removes Richard, the money-raising activity will be time-lagged. Tim's decision map appears in Figure 8-1.

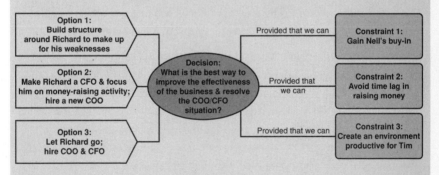

FIGURE 8-1

Tim's Personnel Decision

Tim decides to make Richard the CFO (Option 2).

Tim commented: "When you asked me to find an emotion associated with the decision, I was surprised to find out that it was a threat! Threat!—I thought incredulously. How can it be a threat? It took me awhile to actually understand this, and I will have to think about it some more. But discovering this emotion was extremely instructive.

I realized that this situation needs to be resolved urgently, and that if I do not do it properly, my company, my income, and the work that I love are on the line."

Acknowledging an emotion and then working with it can lead to a decision very quickly, as you can see from the following example.

EXAMPLE 8-3: GENE—RENEGOTIATING A PARTNERSHIP

Gene, a CEO of a marketing services company, is facing "the hardest business decision of his life." Three partners with equal shares started the company 12 years ago; Gene is one of them. The partners have been running the company successfully with the "majority rules" method. In fact, the company is recognized in the media as "one of the most creative and effective marketing firms in the U.S." One partner (Neil) is Gene's closest friend, godfather of his children, and a neighbor. Neil never worked for a large company; he was a freelancer at the start of the company, earning $30,000 per year. The third partner (Steve) worked with Gene at a large telecommunications company, and they both left annual salaries of a quarter-million dollars in order to found this new start-up.

Over the last year, Neil has become ineffective in managing his part of the business and is negative about the company's future. Gene and Steve have decided that the crux of the difficulty is that Neil disagrees with the company's vision. The three of them have put this vision together over the last year. However, Neil did not participate as much as Gene and Steve would have liked. Gene believes that subconsciously Neil knows that his skills do not match the new vision and this is one of the reasons for his unhappiness.

Gene and Steve decided to take an open approach—"Tell us what we can and should change, and let's work it out." After several brainstorming sessions, Neil, unfortunately, did not come back with anything constructive.

This situation has been going on for months, and Gene does not see any resolution. Things are going from bad to worse. He thinks that something needs to be done urgently. One of the options is to buy Neil out, but Gene and Steve believe that somehow they can glue it back together with Neil.

I asked him what he feels about the decision. His answer: "Frustration!" During the time when he contemplates his decision in the Clarity State, he finds a number of other emotions—fear of losing his closest friend if this situation is not resolved positively, anxiety about the status of the business if he allows this limbo state to continue, and excitement about the future of the business if the new vision is executed with passion.

His decision—"It's clear—we should buy Neil out!"

What happened? As Gene says, "The decision was obvious, but all these emotions were standing in the way, and I was unable to move forward because of them. This was the first time when I acknowledged the emotions; you showed me how to deal with them, look them in the face. You also asked me to look at the worst consequences of each outcome, and I realized the damage that I was doing by *not* making a decision. It is far worse than the worst consequences of buying Neil out."

In making his decision, Gene traversed the whole path, from finding various emotions related to the decision and acknowledging them, to facing them by looking at the worst and then realizing the damage of inaction.

Lesson #1 **When you are faced with a difficult decision, make sure you take the time to "discover" an emotion or emotions associated with the situation related to the decision and acknowledge them.**

One of the ways to do this is to ask yourself this question in the Clarity State: "What overriding emotion am I feeling associated with this decision?" Recollect people involved in the situation, their opinions about the decision, the state of the business, and the risk associated with some options. Think about the impact that this decision would make on employees and on you personally. What about your family? In most cases, you are sure to find one or several emotions. Acknowledge them.

Exercise

What are the emotions associated with your decision? Name and list them. You can use the worksheet at the end of this chapter.

The difficulty in the decision you selected might not necessarily be in dealing with emotions. In order for you to benefit from the exercises in this chapter, you may want to select a past decision that was strongly emotional for you.

Shift Negative into Positive

> *Negative emotions are self-limiting. A clear understanding*
> *of negative emotions dismisses them.*
> Chinese proverb

Observation #2: Emotions usually surface unrecognized concerns that should be taken into account in the decision.

After you know what the emotion is, you can use it as a tool. It's associated with a concern that you have not necessarily recognized before. By naming the emotion, you usually find the concern. The best way to start dealing with it is to define it as a constraint and add it to a decision map. In case of emotions, such conversion might present a challenge, as the following example demonstrates.

EXAMPLE 8-4: CARL—STRATEGIC INVESTMENT

Carl is the CEO of a $200 million healthcare products public company. The company's stock has not been doing very well over the last three years. In the last five quarters, however, after the company put itself on an accelerated growth path, and after Carl personally spent time with investment bankers and market makers, its stock has been climbing. Carl is watching the stock price increase with anticipation, because the company is ready for an acquisition. Carl believes, however, that an acquisition should be considered only when the stock price reaches a certain level. He is happy to see that the stock is getting there.

At the moment, Carl is contemplating a product introduction decision. The company has developed and tested a new product. The
product is based on a new concept and is ahead of the competition. The problem is that its introduction will cannibalize the sales
of an existing moneymaking company product. Another problem
is that customers will need to retool in order to utilize the new
product.

Carl is contemplating the risk of this product introduction. Having
learned about the availability of this new product, customers may
decide to stop buying the old product but may not be able to buy
the new one for six months or longer. Therefore, his company's
sales could be hurt significantly, and with it, the stock performance
could be adversely affected too, putting his acquisition plans on
hold. On the other hand, he cannot just hold off the product introduction indefinitely—the competition will surely catch up.

Carl cannot reach the Clarity State, even though he dutifully follows instructions. As he continues to try, Carl is asked to find an
emotion associated with this decision. He realizes that he feels a
high level of anxiety.

In Carl's case, the anxiety is caused partly by his concern about a
significant revenue drop as a result of the product introduction. This
specific concern was already addressed in his decision definition by the
constraint "Minimize negative revenue impact."

Carl shared with me that there is another concern behind the revenue drop, and it is personal. He is afraid that he will make the wrong
call. His incentive program is based on the company's performance.
The targets that the board and he selected are high and almost necessitate an acquisition. If the acquisition does not happen in time, the company will not do as well as he and the board would have liked. He feels
that his position might be on the line with this decision.

According to the process of clarifying constraints, he needs to convert this personal concern into an objective to overcome this concern
using an action verb. This objective can take many forms. He contemplates this conversion in the Clarity State and decides on "Be prepared
to have no increase in salary and no bonus."

Concern:	Constraint:
Making a wrong call	Be prepared to have no increase in salary and no bonus

This is how this conversion happened in his words: "I realized that my career is not really at stake. The reality is that we have to introduce this product soon or we start losing customers. I am not taking the company 'out on a limb' by this decision. The worst that can happen to me personally is negative financial impact. But I think that it would not even come to that."

Stated the new way, the emotion becomes productive. Carl's thinking *shifts* from being in the grip of a negative emotion to a constructive focus of developing strategies to find the right solution. He reaches for data that was put together by the product team that includes projected cannibalization. He immediately sees several ways that the introduction can be managed without the severity of the impact he feared.

Sometimes we become paralyzed at the thought of a difficulty. Instead, we must look for an opportunity in every difficulty. When we do, a creative solution appears. Emotions are effective tools to show us the way.

Exercise

Identify concerns that are causing the emotion or emotions associated with the decision. Convert them into constraints according to the process for clarifying constraints.

It is not a surprise that Carl was unable to reach the Clarity State on the first try. Inability to cope with anxiety is cited as one of the main reasons for athletes' failure to reach the peak performance state. Anxiety is divided into five categories:

- Fear of failure
- Loss of control
- Feeling of inadequacy
- Guilt
- Somatic complaints that are physiological indicators of anxiety, such as sweating, muscle tension, or an upset stomach

It is similar with executives. Anxiety or any other negative emotion can stop you on your way to clarity[10]. Therefore, it is critically important to acknowledge emotions and learn to deal with them constructively.

Lesson #2 Converting unrecognized concern associated with the emotion into a constraint provides a constructive path of benefiting from the emotion.

Learn to Use Physical Sensations as Instruments of Dealing with Emotions

Every emotion has an associated physical sensation in our bodies. Because this statement might seem unusual and "out there," let me explain where it came from. Early on in the research project, one CEO, Bill, told me a story.

EXAMPLE 8-5: BILL—LEAVING A POSITION WITH THE COMPANY

Bill refers to this period as "the most difficult time in my life." Six months ago, a large public software company acquired the company that Bill was running. As a requirement of the deal, Bill became COO of the combined public company. During the due diligence, Bill realized that the two companies had completely different cultures. However, it has taken him these six months since the acquisition to fully understand the degree of the differences. His company had an entrepreneurial culture and was fast to act, with products based on new technology. The public company was spun off from IBM in the mid-'90s. As a result, it had a large organizational structure with products based on older technology, and most people had been with the company for over 20 years. The situation was not helped by the fact that shortly after the acquisition, the company's stock decreased from $20 per share to $4 per share due to the Internet bubble burst.

Many members of Bill's original company's management team were getting frustrated because their financial situation had degraded and because integration decisions were being made with significantly more consideration for the old products and older technology than the new, which they would have preferred. Bill was in constant conflict with the CEO because of these decisions.

A couple of months after the acquisition, Bill developed a pain in his back that was progressively getting worse, so much so that he could not move very well and yelled in pain sometimes while sitting in meetings. He tried physical therapy, drugs, massage, everything he could think of, but nothing helped. He was offered surgery, and everyone advised him to go forward with it. At this critical point in his life, it suddenly became clear to him one morning that his back pain was connected with the fact that "I do not like what we are doing with the company." He decided to leave his position. A month after he left the company, his back was fine.

This story inspired me to do some research on the topic of a connection between emotions and physical pain. I discovered that even though the medical profession does not fully embrace this trend, a number of doctors have accumulated example after example of cases similar to Bill's. They treat these cases by making patients realize that the pain is *caused* by the emotion and then asking patients to find and address the root causes that are creating that emotion in their lives[11,12].

This story was the impetus for starting to ask decision makers not only to find the overriding emotion associated with their decisions but also to find a physical sensation associated with it.

Key Point

All executives who found an emotion associated with the decision also found a physical sensation related to the emotion in their bodies.

In many cases, finding a strong physical sensation associated with an emotion was a major surprise. One person found strong, unpleasant sensations around his heart. He did not know that he had them. They were so intense that he had to stop the meeting and take a break. In the meantime, I started worrying whether he was about to have a heart attack. It took just a couple of brief moments for him to get into the Clarity State and to discover that the outstanding decision had such a severe impact on his body. It is amazing that we often miss such intense signals!

Observation #3: Finding a physical sensation associated with the emotion can serve as an instrument of dealing with the emotion.

I decided to take it a step further and use sensations related to an emotion, which I now realized that people could find, to help decision makers actually deal with these emotions.

My hypothesis was based on a suggestion that a neuroscientist, LeDeoux, made in his writings[4]: "The increased connectivity between the amygdala and the cortex involves fibers going from the cortex to the amygdala as well as from the amygdala to the cortex. If these nerve pathways strike a balance, it is possible that the struggle between thought and emotion may ultimately be resolved not by the dominance of emotional centers by cortical cognitions, but by a more *harmonious integration* (italics added) of reason and passion."

My hypothesis was that, because we cannot totally separate from an emotion, it might be possible to strike this balance or a point of harmonious integration—when emotion is present but to a degree that makes it constructive to the reasoning mechanisms, rather than blocking.

As a result, I asked decision makers to do various visualization exercises and to watch the physical sensation that they found as they were doing the exercises. In all cases (100 percent!), executives reported that the sensation lessened or went away altogether when the right visualization was found! A number of people remarked that the lessening of the sensation allowed them to relax more deeply and contemplate the decision more easily and freely than before.

In Claire's case, the physical sensation went away altogether when she found the right visualization.

PART III

EXAMPLE 8-6: CLAIRE—WHEN SOMEONE BLATANTLY CHEATS YOU, WHAT DO YOU DO?

Claire is the CEO of a specialty food company. Together with a partner, her company developed a product that "took off" on the market. Claire believed that the product's composition needed to be changed to adjust it to the current low carbohydrates trend. Her partner disagreed. After serious contemplation, Claire decided to terminate the agreement with the partner.

She carefully negotiated the exit clause in the contract so that she could make such an exit at a cost that she was willing to accept. When she looked at the signed contract, however, she discovered to her great surprise that several subpoints had been inserted into the exit clause without her knowledge! These points made the contract termination close to impossible. In Claire's words: "I went through a series of emotions, from disbelief to anger to frustration and then to tears."

After pulling out her notes from the time when the contract was under negotiation, Claire became certain that these points were not there at the last revision before the signature. However, she did not keep the pre-signature copies. She only kept her notes. It was possible that she could prove the point in court, but was it worth the pain? She said, "I was stunned that someone would do such a thing!"

Claire found a strong physical sensation associated with all these emotions—an unpleasant sensation in her stomach, "as if I was going to be violently sick." It took her several tries to finally identify a visualization that lessened the sensation. She imagined a scene in which she talked to the principal of the other company who negotiated the contract with her. In that scene, he admitted to her that he had changed one page in the contract just before it was signed. Nobody noticed. He also explained why he did that. Claire's feedback: "The scene was imaginary, but it felt real. I suddenly realized that he cheated out of desperation—to keep us in business together because this product was a great moneymaker for his company. Without wanting to, I forgave him at that very instant. The sensation in the stomach went away completely."

The end of the story is positive. Claire confronted the partner's principal, and they negotiated an amicable termination of the contract. You gain strength, courage, and confidence by every experience in which you really stop to look a negative emotion in the face. The danger lies in refusing to face the emotion, in not daring to come to grips with it. When you dare, you find a way to deal with the emotion and convert it into a positive tool in your decision-making. Push yourself to succeed every time, and find a way to do what you think you cannot do.

Observation #3a: Effective visualizations that lessen a physical sensation associated with the decision can help strike a balance between emotion and reason to enable easier decision-making.

In other words, this is how physical indications (sensations) can be used to deal with emotions. Because we know that we cannot fully separate from an emotion, we should focus on striking a balance between emotion and reason.

What does this mean—striking a balance between emotion and reason? Actually, we all know the answer, because all of us have experienced this balance in our decision-making, but let me try to state it.

At one end of the spectrum is the point when the emotion is totally blocking you from making a decision (as in the case of Gene's decision). On the other end of the spectrum is the point when you really do not care at all. The balance is found in the middle, when you are feeling that you care, you are involved, but you can review the situation without giving in to the emotion and instead are taking it into account.

PART III

Lesson #3   **When you are faced with a difficult decision, make sure that you not only find an emotion associated with the situation related to the decision and acknowledge it, but also find a physical sensation associated with this emotion. Work with visualization exercises, and select the one that lessens the physical sensation. Use it as an instrument to find the right level of emotion for *balanced* decision contemplation.**

In some sense, this is nothing new—we all know the old dictum of "detach" when you are faced with a strong emotion related to a decision. But how? If you are emotionally involved in the situation, how do you detach? As LeDoux says: "Although thoughts can easily trigger emotions (by activating the amygdala), we are not very effective at willfully turning off emotions (by deactivating the amygdala). Telling yourself that you should not be anxious or depressed does not help very much[4]."

The described method provides a "handle," or an instrument that can help you achieve the right level of detachment from emotions. By using this instrument, the method provides a way for us to *observe* how our actions change our emotional state.

> ### Exercise
> Identify physical sensations associated with the acknowledged emotion or emotions related to your decision.

Find a Balance Point by Using Visualizations

> *The heart has its reasons that reason does not know.*
> Pascal[13]

Attachment is the greatest fabricator of illusion. Reality can be attained only by someone who is detached. You can get detached by working with your emotions. Every emotion is a thought transformed into feeling. Change the thought that creates this emotion, and you can look at a situation in a more detached manner.

The following are several effective visualization exercises for finding a balance point between emotion and reason. They incorporate ideas from CEOs running large companies who have learned ways to strike this balance when they are contemplating difficult decisions.

As you are working with these visualizations, monitor the sensation in your body that you associated with this situation. Is the feeling gone, or is it less intense? If so, you have found the right visualization. Continue to work with it until you feel that you can look at the situation from the "outside in" perspective.

You might want to assign a symbol to the situation related to the decision. The first thing that comes to mind is probably the right symbol. You can use this symbol as you do these visualizations.

Practice #1: Visualizing Distance Between Yourself and the Decision

Put the situation related to your decision far away from you (for example, imagine that you are standing on the beach and this situation is on the horizon somewhere), and then bring it close; do this a couple of times. The effect you want to achieve is that your emotional connection to this situation is getting weaker and weaker and you feel strong, independent of whatever happens with the situation.

Practice #2: Physically Separating from the Decision

There are a number of ways to do this. It's limited by your imagination. Be creative—find the way that works for you.

A: Put the decision in a box, and lose the key to the box. Imagine a funny scene as you are looking for the key.

B: Put the decision in a balloon, and let it fly away. See yourself standing in a beautiful field with the balloon slowly flying away from you, carrying your decision away.

C: Imagine that you and the decision are connected by many lines. Imagine that you are cutting all these lines with scissors.

D: Imagine that you are writing the decision on a blackboard and then wiping it clean.

Practice #3: Giving the Problem to Someone Else

Imagine that you are consulting someone else on this issue. It is not your issue any more; it's this person's. After you finish the discussion, imagine that you stand up and walk out of the room, leaving the other person with this problem.

Practice #4: Simply Letting Go

Simply state to yourself: "I now let go of this situation and all the burden that it has been for me." And simply let go.

> ### Exercise
>
> Work with visualizations (these and your own) to identify an emotional balance point. Finding this vantage point will be critical in the next two parts of the process—finding a clear perspective and aligning with outcomes. Write down the most effective visualizations you developed.

The following process of effectively dealing with emotions summarizes observations and lessons learned here and will help you constructively work with strong emotions that might be related to your decision.

The Process of Dealing with Emotions in Decision-Making

- Reach the Clarity State.
- Find an emotion or emotions associated with the situation related to the decision. Acknowledge them.
- Shift the emotion into a constructive, positive statement by formulating the concern that is causing the emotion as a constraint in your decision definition. The process for clarifying decision constraints will necessitate that the concern related to the emotion is converted into a subobjective to *overcome* the concern.
- Find a physical sensation associated with the emotion.
- Use the physical sensation as an instrument to find the emotional balance point. Work with visualization exercises, and select the one that lessens the physical sensation.

Emotions are part of us and are present in our decisions, like it or not. Unfortunately, business schools do not teach us how to deal with them in the decision-making process, and literature on the subject is sparse. We all have to spend a large part of our careers developing our own techniques of working with emotions. The simple yet powerful techniques offered in this chapter can help you in decision situations when you are under the spell of a negative emotion that is tough to deal with.

Worksheet 8-1: Dealing with Emotions

Emotion:

Concern causing the emotion:

Constraint—objective to overcome the concern:

1. _____

2. _____

3. _____

CHAPTER 9

Pick a Fight!—How to Get the Most Out of Clashing Opinions

When dealing with people, remember you are not dealing with creatures of logic, but with creatures of emotion.
Dale Carnegie[1]

Disagreements add an extra level of emotions to what is sometimes an already emotionally charged and complex situation.

When your team doubts your reasoning, for example, it is tough not to be affected by the doubts. You start doubting your decision yourself. Reaching clarity becomes more difficult, especially if you are not an autocratic manager, but rather one who requires unanimous agreement from your team before proceeding with a strategic move. Proceeding with a decision despite a disagreement requires an extra level of self-confidence and belief in your vision. This is why, as a norm, managers try to avoid disagreements[2]. Disagreements have the potential to be confrontational or emotional and, even worse, to change a working team into a dysfunctional one.

However, effective leaders encourage disagreement[3]. They know that the truth is born in the clash of divergent opinions. Concerns are raised and creative solutions are developed. *In fact, effective leaders create contention on purpose.* Franklin Roosevelt was known to ask subordinates who he knew had different perspectives on an issue to work on it "in strictest confidence." He knew perfectly well that such secret assignments would immediately become known to other people, thus creating a contentious environment.

Key Point
Disagreements can be used as a tool to get to clarity faster.

This chapter discusses several best practices that will help you create and handle disagreements as well as emotions associated with them in order to get to clarity of your decision faster.

Assignment

If the decision you selected in Chapter 1, "The Key to Mastering Decisions," does not have a disagreement involved, choose another current or past decision that has this dynamic. Write it down in your notebook.

As you go through the chapter, apply the best practices to the chosen situation. Write down your observations. How do you usually handle disagreements? What can you do differently next time you encounter a disagreement?

Constructive Use of Disagreements

No one is thinking if everyone is thinking alike.
George S. Patton[4]

Disagreements create emotionally challenging situations, but they can be *constructive* if handled properly[5].

Let me quote one CEO: "I find that, when people disagree, they do not take the time to formulate specifics of the disagreement. With time, the disagreeing parties stop communicating effectively, and layers of emotional resentment are added on top of the initial disagreement. But, in fact, if they were to focus on the root causes constructively and define them clearly to their mutual satisfaction, this step alone would have shifted the parties into the mode of looking for a solution."

Best Practice #1   Insist on clearly defining root causes of the disagreement to the mutual satisfaction of the disagreeing parties.

In Example 7-3 in Chapter 7, "Escaping Handcuffs—How to Achieve Clarity of Constraints," Lin worked on a strategy to achieve a tight integration with customers through better information technology capability. He incorporated concerns raised by his objecting team members about a proposed strategy into the decision definition and in doing so provided a way to effectively address the concerns.

Let's look at another example to demonstrate how areas of disagreement can be clearly defined and incorporated into the decision definition.

PART III

EXAMPLE 9-1: ERIC—ACQUISITION DECISION

Eric is the CEO of a software company. His company is considering an acquisition in Europe. Eric is facing a decision whether to go forward with the acquisition or not.

The difficulty is that the VP of Marketing and the CFO, who was responsible for the due diligence process, disagree. The CFO has command of the facts by nature of being close to the situation. He recommends proceeding with the acquisition. The VP of Marketing, on the other hand, sees danger signs in the market acceptance of the target's main product by customers. He believes that the demand is softening and will actually drop sharply later on. This potential future scenario was not taken into consideration in financial projections related to the acquisition. If it were to occur after the acquisition is completed, the impact on the combined company could be profound.

In addition, there is a strategic "mismatch"—the target company has been evolving its products in a certain direction, opposite to Eric's company. This situation creates a strategic dilemma.

Contemplating the situation in the Clarity State, Eric realized that he was biased. He wanted to complete the acquisition against all odds. In his words, "I was hit with the realization that I knew about the mismatch from the very beginning. I was just hoping that somehow we would find a way to make it a go. After all, the mere revenue addition to our company would be a huge advantage. I also realized that we did not define the objective clearly initially—I did not put my brightest people on the team and I did not ask for detailed updates throughout the due diligence process. Here I am facing an irreversible decision, we wasted tons of resources on it, and I totally mismanaged the whole thing!"

Eric decided to listen to all opinions. He told me that if a solution could be found so that the acquisition could proceed, so be it. If it became clear that the only feasible choice was to cancel the acquisition, he was ready to face the situation of losing face with the target, with his team, and with his board.

A meeting with all concerned followed. Eric made it a focus of the meeting to surface concerns at a detailed level and to generate ideas about potentially resolving them. Solutions were not obvious, especially in the area of integrating two main products of the corresponding companies to satisfy emerging customer needs. The disagreement between the VP of Marketing and the CFO was rooted in the differences in their corresponding assessments of the future market needs and development. Eric continuously focused the team, including participants from the target company, on "stating the facts," pinpointing the area of disagreement, understanding the basis behind it, and finding a solution.

The team finally agreed on two main concerns:

1. If the acquisition proceeded, both sets of customer needs as envisioned by corresponding companies would need to be satisfied. It was not clear how, however. There was no easy way to integrate divergent main products to make the combined product address both sets of needs.

2. Was the softening of the customer demand for the target's product real? If it was, what could the combined company do about it?

The team's agreed-upon decision definition appears in Figure 9-1.

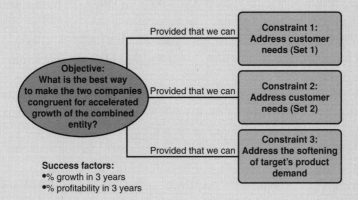

FIGURE 9-1

Eric's Team Decision Definition

It took several days to figure out potential viable solutions. It was clear that the concerns could be addressed, but with additional resources. At the end of the day, Eric's team proposed an acquisition price reduction in order to address the raised concerns in the integration strategy. Fortunately for Eric and his team, the acquisition target accepted the offer at that price level.

To summarize, the process of identifying root causes behind disagreement and incorporating them into a decision has the following steps:

1. Formulate areas of agreement as well as disagreement, and be specific about them. Ask the objecting side(s) to do the same independently, compare notes, and pinpoint the differences clearly. State the facts.

2. Convert the areas of concern into constraints by working as a team.

3. Make sure that you have a collective decision definition that captures concerns of both parties.

4. Contemplate the decision in the Clarity State, and ask each person involved in the disagreement to do the same. Then discuss the results. Focus the discussion on structuring creative solutions to address the objective and constraints.

In the case of Eric's team, this process focused everyone on the same critical-to-the-business objective and channeled the energy into developing a solution acceptable to both sides. By his leadership, Eric converted a dysfunctional situation into a focused effort of achieving the required result.

Eric told me that the whole situation made him review his priorities and his process of attending to them. When disagreements surface late in a critical project, as in this case, it is useful to ask yourself a simple question: "What could I/we have done differently throughout the process that could have led to a different result?"

In Eric's case, the disagreement was apparent. Eric could have learned more about the disagreement by just encouraging an open discussion about concerns. However, we often find ourselves in situations when our intuition tells us "something is wrong," but we lack information to make an independent judgment.

Best Practice #2 **Create contention to learn more about potential vulnerabilities underlying the decision. Contention stimulates imagination.**

Here is how one CEO did it.

EXAMPLE 9-2: MARC—BUSINESS TURNAROUND

Marc was asked to become the CEO of a technology company whose CEO had left. During the first month, Marc discovered serious problems with the business. As he was doing the initial business situation assessment, it was becoming clear to him that the Internet and other market dynamics would eventually eliminate the revenue of the whole subdivision that was currently responsible for half of the business.

Members of his staff, on the other hand, were unwilling to face the issue, denying such a possibility—a situation that was frustrating to Marc. In the long run, he needed to put together a turnaround plan. In the short term, he felt that a significant layoff was required to offset the revenue risk.

The difficulty in this decision was that Marc had no previous experience in this industry. He felt that he was "running blind," especially without the total cooperation and buy-in of his staff. The decision was emotional because of the fear of making a wrong move and the risk to his career that such a move would entail.

Marc put together what he calls a "devil's advocate" meeting by asking a group of people knowledgeable in the business to propose a solution for the short-term and long-term strategy and invited another group to critique the proposal.

Marc was there but in an observer capacity, not as a participant. This meeting allowed him to obtain a deeper understanding of the issues as they were hashed out in front of him. It enabled him to proceed with a 20 percent layoff.

The situation is not unlike many that executives have to handle when they join a nonperforming company. In fact, a new executive expects to find fires on all fronts. As a result of being new, Marc was not emotionally vested in the situation because he did not create the problems and could not be blamed for them. Therefore, he was able to stay detached from the emotional outbursts of others who were vested in the situation and to handle them effectively.

By creating contention and disagreement, he was able to gain a better grasp of the business issues and weigh his personal opinions against the realities of the situation.

In summary, one way to create contention is to

- Identify people who know "long-timers" in the business from different angles of its operation. Create a task group.

- Ask them to make a recommendation on a particular strategic business issue.

- Collect a group of other highly experienced people, and have a "devil's advocate" meeting where these people identify a fault with the proposal of the task group.

- Do not participate in the discussion, but be there and listen carefully. Write down your own questions and run proposed ideas against your gut. Often, you become certain about the right way to proceed as a result of such meetings.

Best Practice #3   Put yourself in an observer mode.

Notice that Marc gained more from the discussion because he was *an observer,* not a participant. It was possible for him to be in the observer capacity because he was new to the company. Obviously, this is harder to do when you are vested in the decision as much as other participants or even more. In such cases, bring in an outside facilitator to get you "off the hook" and collect opinions in a nonthreatening way. A skilled facilitator can give you the gift of being allowed to observe, collect information, and even participate in a neutral role.

Everybody wants something from the decision maker. Realize that all people have their own biases and are always looking to get a decision that they favor, in most cases in good faith, without knowing that they are biased. Creating contention and disagreement in those cases helps identify biases and safeguards you against becoming a prisoner to them.

Best Practice #4   Use disagreements to safeguard against being the prisoner of the organization's or someone else's biases.

Here is how Kevin used a disagreement that helped him identify a specific perspective that his whole organization was operating under, change it, and arrive at a decision agreeable to all.

EXAMPLE 9-3: KEVIN—LAYOFF CANDIDATE SELECTION

Kevin took the role of CEO on an invitation from an investment banker to "fix" the failing company. The first order of business was to execute a significant layoff. As Kevin was reviewing recommendations of layoff candidates from each function and asking for cross-functional feedback, he observed that there was a disagreement about the layoff in the sales organization. There was no disagreement about the need to lay off one of the five regional sales managers. The disagreement was about which one.

Kevin decided to interview all regional managers. He observed that the manager of the West Coast region exhibited behaviors that he personally associated with a commonly failing management style, which adheres to an "us versus them" mentality and a dictatorial approach. If it were Kevin's personal choice, he would have laid off that manager. The VP of Sales, however, recommended a different regional manager for the layoff. His reasoning was based on the fact that the performance of the West Coast region had been good.

After a discussion with the VP of Sales, Kevin was in doubt and decided to talk to other team members to get their opinions indirectly. It appeared that his view was supported, and, in fact, he heard complaints about the difficulty of working with the West Coast region.

Kevin did not want to appear dictatorial and demand his way with the VP of Sales. He was faced with a dilemma. He decided to look at this situation in the Clarity State. Here is his feedback: "I suddenly realized that I am imposing a 'values' constraint on the selection of the layoff candidates. This constraint states that I want people in the company who align with specific values, and only such employees would grow within the company. The problem was that I was not telling anybody about this requirement. Therefore, the VP of Sales continued to operate within the historically acceptable frame—'performance is all that matters.'"

The rest was easy. Kevin was able to clearly communicate his additional values requirement to the team. He decided to finalize the layoff list across functions at a staff meeting and discuss this particular issue. At that meeting, the VP of Sales changed his recommendation about the layoff candidate based on the feedback from his peers and Kevin's new requirement.

Often, the difficulty of a decision springs from the fact that you are not close to the situation and its details. At the point of the decision, you might feel doubtful about the rightness of the decision if people close to the situation disagree with your view.

In conflict with people on a decision, the crux of the difficulty has to be defined, evaluated, and resolved before proceeding with the final choice. In Kevin's case, the disagreement helped him identify the organizational frame that people were operating under, which was different from his own. This realization resolved the disagreement and united the organization on a particular choice.

Notice that Kevin used another effective process that one CEO calls "feeding your gut"—indirectly or directly collecting additional information about a certain preferred path. Kevin felt that this process allowed him to clarify his own views and then figure out the crux of the issue. He admits that he felt strongly about his initial desire to lay off the West Coast regional manager. Getting additional information and confirming that his view was supported helped him handle these emotions.

If approached constructively, disagreements can be extremely useful on the path to decision clarity[6]. A disagreement can help you surface important parameters related to the decision, stimulate imagination in developing alternative solutions, and safeguard you against biases and frames. Welcome disagreements when they exist; create them when they do not. You are more likely to arrive at clarity faster.

Disagreements and Emotions

If you welcome disagreements, you will need to welcome emotions that come with them. Unfortunately, these emotions are usually unpleasant. You are likely to experience resistance, anger, and impatience to get to the result you want, to name just a few[7].

You will find that your attitude is everything in dealing with disagreements.

> **Best Practice #5** Watch your attitude. Make sure that you truly welcome the disagreement.

If you view the presence of a disagreement as a curse, you will experience negative emotions and will be unlikely to reap positive benefits that we discussed earlier. If you truly welcome disagreements and divergent opinions, you will find solutions easier. In fact, sometimes it will seem that problems resolve themselves. *Treat any disagreement as a gift that will speed up the decision and improve its quality.*

By its very nature of being a high, positive state, the Clarity State can help you find this emotional stance of welcoming a particular disagreement. Here is a visualization you can use:

- Get into the Clarity State.
- Imagine your team sitting in a circle around you. Tell them mentally that you welcome their input and would like everyone to work on the constructive resolution of this particular situation. Describe your vision and how this decision contributes to this vision. Invite opinions.
- See yourself being open to these opinions, listening to them carefully and asking questions. You do not contradict or restate your view. Just listen.
- See people open up and contribute more ideas. Creativity soars.
- Feel positive energy from this interchange. Be there and live it.
- Imagine a timeline to a successful resolution of the issue. Now, imagine that it shrinks in half. Reduce it some more to the point that you are comfortable.

PART III

Be creative. You can develop other effective visualizations. The intent is to become open, to overcome your resistance to other people's opinions.

In all these examples, the decision makers were in control. Even though disagreements that complicated decisions were present, these decision makers could have proceeded without getting their teams on-board. This is not the case when a decision maker disagrees with his boss or a CEO disagrees with the board.

Best Practice #6 In situations where you have limited control, remind yourself that you are a recommender, not a decider. This attitude will allow you to find the emotional balance point easier.

Let me give you an example.

EXAMPLE 9-4: ED—DISAGREEMENT WITH THE BOARD

Ed is the CEO of a software company. His company is three years old and just received a large buyout offer. Ed needs to make a recommendation to the board concerning whether this offer should be accepted. The difficulty in making a recommendation is that Ed knows that the board is deadlocked on this issue.

His company's plan is to file IPO in a year or so. The valuations in the market are high.

The situation is complicated by the fact that his company was spun off by a multibillion-dollar public company as a joint venture with a partner—another multibillion-dollar company. The board is evenly split between representatives of the parent company and the partner. The parent company is against the sale, and the partner is for it.

Ed considered this situation in the Clarity State. One realization helped him make the decision. He realized that he had limited control over the decision, even though he had strong beliefs about what was the right choice. The decision was with the board, and his function was to clearly articulate his reasoning to the board. This realization helped him make the decision.

Ed says that this realization enabled him to become more balanced emotionally. He focused on communicating his concerns to the board—the already apparent softening of the IPO market, future required cash infusions, inadequate investment into new product development, and others.

He decided to recommend taking the offer. At the meeting, the parent company's board members were able to convince several directors from the partner's company that, even though the offer is great, the IPO would make more money. The board decided to decline the offer.

Ed was vested in the company financially and emotionally. He said, "I felt that since I was certain that I was right, I should have been able to find a way to convince the board that my path was correct. I still feel that I failed because I was unable to do it."

The story does not have a good ending. The market for IPOs softened shortly after the board decision, and the company could not file for an IPO in time. The board members who opposed the sale realized that they should reconsider their decision. However, the buyer was no longer interested. In the end, the parent company had to buy back the share from the partner. All investors lost money.

The same realization of limited control helped Fred deal with the major disagreement in his start-up, as described in the following example. Fred had limited control over the decision, too, even though his disagreement was not with the board but with an equal partner.

PART III

EXAMPLE 9-5: FRED—DISAGREEMENT WITH A PARTNER

Fred started his company with his friend as an equal partner a couple of years ago. They realized that they needed a general manager to run the business on a day-to-day basis. They hired Dan, who worked for Fred previously. Dan's arrival brought the company to a new level. Sales increased dramatically, and the business started prospering.

Fred's partner proposed that the company make Dan a partner. Fred did not see any reason to do so because Dan was doing well and was well paid. He did not feel that they owed Dan such a position. In addition, such a move would complicate the existing survivorship and life insurance policy issues. However, his partner was stuck on this issue, fearing that Dan might decide to leave them and start his own business or retire. In that case, their company might not survive.

The partners spent months debating.

Fred contemplated this decision in the Clarity State and was surprised by his own choice. He decided to agree with his partner. Dan is now a minority owner of the business.

What happened?

Fred said that it was the realization of the limited control that was most instrumental in making him look at the situation from a different angle. He then realized that making his partner happy was critical for the success of their business. "I felt that my partner's concerns were purely emotionally based, but nonetheless I needed to address them." Fred also realized that making Dan a partner would only increase Dan's desire to accelerate the company's growth.

This example is common for start-ups. I listened to a number of cases that were almost exactly like Fred's. In a disagreement of two equal partners in a start-up, the decision often becomes emotional and trying on the relationship, especially if two partners are friends. There is a Chinese proverb: "Never engage in business with friends."

Best Practice #7 In situations where you have equal control over the decision shared with another party, agree with the other party on the strategy of selection between outcomes before a major disagreement develops.

When equal partners disagree after opinions have been aired but no apparent solution is found to resolve the disagreement, you can handle such situations constructively if you have a prior agreement on *a strategy of selection* between outcomes. Some partners agree on the selection process at the start of the venture. Some select the method of flipping a coin. Some adopt a process of pursuing one partner's choice, assuming that at the next disagreement, they will follow the other partner's solution.

In cases of disagreement, communicating the reasoning to the objecting party is a critical component to reaching clarity. Communication played a critical role to resolution in all previous examples.

Spending time on developing a separate decision layer focused on communications will provide extra clarity about potential solutions. This layer is different from the decision itself. Techniques for doing this separation are discussed in Appendix B, "Additional Tips on Reducing Decision Complexity."

Best Practice #8 Separate your decision from the communication of the decision. Focus on communications. Be clear about your intent, your motivation, the business need, and other important factors of the decision.

This best practice is critically important. Communication prior to the decision and about the decision can be as important as the decision itself. Pay attention to what you are communicating. Use Clarity State to spell out and sharpen your message.

In a disagreement, you are likely to feel resistance to the ideas and solutions from the other party. It is important to check whether the issue of disagreement goes against your values. If it does, you will have no choice but to communicate this fact to the other party.

You cannot execute a decision that goes against your values. The other party understands this, too. The mere realization that an issue of disagreement goes against your values may shift the situation into a constructive discussion.

Best Practice #9 Be true to yourself. Take a stance if the issue of disagreement goes against your values.

In the following example, Jill's realization that a situation was tied to her values enabled her to make a clear choice—it became a matter of principle for her.

PART III

EXAMPLE 9-6: JILL—HANDLING A SEXUAL HARASSMENT CASE

Jill runs a large medical center. Several months ago, she received five complaints about Pat, the Chief of Emergency. All complaints related to sexual harassment. The incidents were small, such as making inappropriate sexual comments about customers, or looking over the person's shoulder in the restroom. However, Jill was alarmed. Previously, she noticed various performance issues in Pat's department and discussed them with him. Thus, this was the "straw that broke the camel's back." After learning about the latest incidents, she felt that Pat should not be in this critical job.

She discussed the issue at the board and found resistance from two directors who did not want her to pursue any action against Pat. Jill suggested that she would consult two legal firms and follow their advice. Both firms advised her to write a strong letter warning Pat that he would lose his job if the situation were repeated. At the next board meeting, when the issue of the letter came up, both directors advised her not to send it.

This was a difficult decision for Jill. She said that she spent "countless hours" worrying about it. In a clarity moment, she realized that if she did not send the letter, she "would not like herself." She felt that it was "a matter of principle."

This realization was a liberating experience. She felt that it enabled her to take the stance and defend her values and her integrity. She realized at that moment that she was willing to accept the worst-case scenario—to sacrifice her position with the company and her financial stability. Irrespective of that, she felt that she had to "set the record straight." "I had to take a stance; otherwise, I would not be able to live with myself," she said.

Jill embarked on a communication strategy with the board members. She carefully explained her position and her decision. She was able to gain unanimous agreement this time. Jill sent the letter, and Pat left the company shortly afterwards.

Jill knew that this was the right decision when she sent the letter. The rightness of the decision was additionally confirmed later when Pat's replacement found financial reporting irregularities in the emergency department—a situation that Jill had previously suspected.

You might remember a case discussed in an earlier chapter. In Example 3-3, George dealt with a disagreement with investment bankers on his board by leaving the company. His reason for leaving was also a matter of principle. He did not believe in the financial strategy that the investment bankers were insisting on and that he was asked to execute by the board.

Unlike George, having realized the root cause of the disagreement, Jill was able to develop a mutually agreeable action plan through effective communication with the board members. The situation was resolved, and she did not have to sacrifice her position, as George had to.

Sometimes, after having tried everything you can think of to resolve a disagreement, it remains. You are out of time, and the decision has to be made. Well, this is the situation that justifies your salary. It's your call. Use the Clarity State to make the decision that is right for you using the process defined in this book. Then focus on the communications layer. Focus on uniting the team, pointing out to them that you considered their opinions and took them into account. Substantiate your decision to the best of your ability.

In summary, disagreements can be a powerful tool in the hands of a master decision maker on the path to clarity. When handled properly, they can surface critical parameters related to the decision, safeguard against wrong frames, and stimulate imagination. In situations where you feel that you need more information, create a disagreement.

Dealing with disagreements requires a higher level of emotional balance, however. The following process of effectively dealing with disagreements summarizes best practices mentioned earlier and will help you constructively work with disagreements as a tool to get to clarity faster.

PART III

Process of Dealing with Disagreements in Decision-Making

There can be no reconciliation where there is no open warfare. There must be a battle, a brave, boisterous battle, with pennants waving and cannon roaring, before there can be peaceful treaties and enthusiastic shaking of hands.
Mary Elizabeth Braddon[8]

- **Welcome the disagreement.** Look at the whole situation as a gift that will get you and others to clarity faster. Use the Clarity State to find this emotional stance.

- **Define the disagreement.** Insist on clearly defining root causes of the disagreement to the mutual satisfaction of the disagreeing parties. Use the Clarity State decision definition process.

- **Create a communications layer for your decision.** Use techniques presented in Appendix B. Effective communication is your tool for learning more about the situation as well as bringing divergent parties together.

- **Put yourself in an observer capacity.** Extricate yourself from being in the middle of a disagreement. Bring in a third party to facilitate. Collect additional opinions in a nonthreatening way.

- **Identify assumptions and biases** of parties involved, including yourself. Ask each party to list biases of the other parties. Leverage Clarity State for this identification. Ask each party to review these biases in the Clarity State using the technique presented in Chapter 11, "Becoming a Frame Artist—How to Master Clarity of Perspective."

- **Be true to yourself.** Be open to opinions of others, but do not compromise your values.

- **Know your role.** In cases of limited control, remind yourself that you are a recommender, not a decider. Strive for agreement on the resolution process.

- **Insist on a constructive approach.** Use disagreement to develop creative solutions by using the imagination and visualization techniques of Chapter 12, "Bull's-eye!—How to Align with the Right Outcome."

Exercise

Select a situation that involved a disagreement that you did not handle as well as you would have liked. What would you have done differently? Replay the situation in your mind. But this time, imagine that it went according to your new plan, completing in a resolution that you like.

Which of the new actions that you applied in resolving the disagreement this time are worth adopting for your arsenal of best practices in future decision-making?

CHAPTER 10

Everything Is Relative!—Why the Right Frame Is Critical

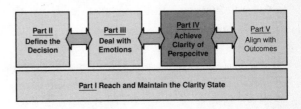

Mastery comes most readily to those who look with the eyes of a beginner, and it comes with great difficulty to those who assume they already know.
Nicholas Lore[1]

By its nature, any decision perspective is limiting. It puts a decision into a frame, highlighting certain elements and hiding the rest. A wrong decision perspective presents a major difficulty in arriving at a clear choice. Effective executives are "frame busters" and "frame artists." They know that decision frames are partly controlled by the formulation of the problem and partly by the norms, habits, and characteristics of the decision maker[2]. They also know that we rarely spontaneously question the formulation of a problem or the underlying personal or business assumptions behind our current perspective. We rarely reframe instinctively.

Key Point

In order to reach clarity on a decision faster and easier, learn to be a frame artist—be able to quickly reframe.

Are You Framed?

In the following example, Brian is dealing with a frame imposed by historical business patterns.

EXAMPLE 10-1: BRIAN—SELECTING A VENDOR

Brian is the new CEO of a company that provides power to several states. His organization is part of a very large utility company. A large contract ($50 million) is currently under renegotiation. This contract is for the maintenance of the power reactor system installed at the plants under his management.

The current maintenance vendor ("Current Vendor") was the original developer and provider of the installed system. Brian's company has never changed vendors. As was expected in this situation, the Current Vendor's price is rather high. Brian sees the situation as "We are being held for ransom on the price." The Current Vendor is known to never change prices under customer pressure.

The competing vendor is a reputable company but with no history of working with Brian's firm. The risk of switching vendors is high—if something unexpected were to happen, the downtime could cost Brian's company $300,000 a day.

It has been decided to take the decision to the operating board, a meeting of all the officers of the company. The Vice Chairman of the parent company usually runs the meeting. After some discussion, the Vice Chairman asks for each person's opinion,

Brian being the last person. The opinion so far is unanimous to award the contract to the Current Vendor at their proposed price.

It is now Brian's turn. He says, "I strongly believe that the Current Vendor will 'cave in' on the price if we pressure them. You should personally call them and tell them that we are awarding the contract to the other vendor." The Vice Chairman calls the Current Vendor's CEO with all the officers watching him. At the end of the five-minute conversation, the Current Vendor's CEO proposes a package reduced by $10 million.

What happened?

All the officers of the company had prior history with the current vendor and believed that the current vendor had never changed its pricing in negotiations, especially not while under pressure. They were operating under an assumption: "Current vendor does not negotiate."

What did Brian know that other officers did not know? He had learned that the CEO of the current vendor would be retiring soon. Brian concluded that the CEO probably did not want to lose a major customer and a major contract before his retirement. It happened that the Vice Chairman paid attention to the same piece of information as Brian did and had the same perspective as Brian.

In the current environment, the stated assumption about the current vendor was wrong. But the rest of the executives were framed by the presence of this perceived constraint in the problem definition. If Brian and his Vice Chairman did not reframe, the company would have overpaid $10 million for the contract.

You have already worked with identifying assumptions behind your decision in the process of clarifying constraints. The techniques in the next chapter will help you identify assumptions and other constraints that are false.

Frames come from two main sources. First, frames come from the way the problem is presented to you. It might be tinted with other parties' opinions, media expectations, and other environmental factors. Second, frames come from unrecognized personal and business assumptions, attitudes, and habits. Whatever the source, you should always be on the lookout for framing factors.

Good Practice for a Frame Buster
Always assume that you are framed.
Be on the lookout for framing factors.

> **Exercise**
>
> Taking into account the main sources of frames discussed here, list framing factors that might be affecting your chosen decision.
>
> Who presented the problem to you? How does the overall environment affect the situation? What main assumptions (business and personal) are you making? What is the difference between how your company would approach the resolution of this problem versus another organization—a nonprofit, for example? List as many framing factors as you can.

Value of a Clear Perspective

A man who is very busy seldom changes his opinions.

Friedrich Nietzsche[3]

The value of identifying the appropriate frame is enormous. Finding the appropriate decision perspective can point to the right solution, identify additional options, and help you identify a problem area or block in relation to the decision.

Value 1: Clear Perspective Points to the Right Solution

Finding the appropriate frame of reference can point to the most appropriate option—making the decision clear in an instant, as you can see from the following example.

EXAMPLE 10-2: STUART—COMPLETING CONSTRUCTION OF TWO NEW PLANTS

Stuart just took the position of CEO of a large manufacturing company. His predecessor left a month prior to Stuart's arrival, and there was no one in the top position during the interim. During the interview process, Stuart was told about a critical project that was not going well. He knew that his first matter of business would be to fix the situation. What he did not know was how bad the situation had gotten.

His company was building two plants to satisfy large orders from several customers. Construction was critically dependent on delivery of certain equipment by a vendor on a specific schedule. When Stuart arrived, the relationship with the vendor was in its sixth month out of 15 months to final delivery. Only three of 10 scheduled equipment installations were conducted by the vendor without issues. By now, the vendor realized that it had committed to a schedule that was unrealistic. The terms of the initial contract and whether the vendor was in breach were being argued between both sides by the lawyers.

Financially, the impact of not getting the plants operational on time was dramatic. If Stuart's company did not start production on time, it would lose over half a million dollars per plant per day.

In addition, there was disagreement internally between two functions, manufacturing and engineering, on how the situation could be resolved. When Stuart arrived, the disagreement between two functional VPs had reached "war" level.

Stuart decided to have a meeting with two functional VPs individually first. He asked each one of them to clearly define the root causes behind the disagreement with the other VP. After listening to their definitions, several concerns came out. The main issue was buried in the design of the new manufacturing lines at the plants under construction. The manufacturing VP had a serious concern about the level of product quality that could be consistently achieved with the current design. The design of the lines was "pushing the envelope" in terms of product quality output to a point where the company had no previous experience. The disagreement between VPs was rooted in the differences between their corresponding assessments of the future results. In order to verify the design, the engineering group needed specific test data that the manufacturing was not providing fully due to the problems with the vendor's equipment delivery.

The same week, Stuart had a meeting with the vendor's CEO, armed with the history of the situation from his company's side. He focused the meeting on the question "How will we make this a success?" He was not surprised when the other CEO brought up a number of issues on Stuart's company's side that allegedly had prevented the vendor from installing equipment on time and with quality.

During the exercise, Stuart realized that the most important aspect of the situation was the eventual *consistent delivery of quality product* in the two plants. The current plan could not guarantee it. His decision was contrary to the expectations of the various parties involved, risky and gutsy: "Stop construction until we have a clear plan to deliver quality products."

The story ends well—both plants started production on time, and "quality is so far, so good." Under Stuart's leadership, the engineering team took some of the state-of-the-art, untested functionality from the design of the manufacturing line, enabling the vendor and the manufacturing group to deliver the project on time.

Value 2: Clear Perspective Identifies Additional Options

One major implication of operating in a "frame" is a difficulty in seeing other solution options or other ways of resolving the situation that may be open at the time[2]. A "frame" blinds you to other choices. Consider the following example.

EXAMPLE 10-3: JANE—LOSING A MAJOR CUSTOMER

Jane's company (CL) works in partnership with several hardware manufacturers to service government agencies with specialized educational software. Usually, Jane's company is the lead on deals with prospects, and the hardware partners follow the lead. One of her hardware partners decided not to work with Jane's company on the last large deal and signed the deal directly with the customer. Jane's question is, "What do we do next to win the customer back?"

Several difficulties are involved in this decision. The customer, a state agency, commands a large percentage (40 percent) of the state's budget. This agency has been CL's customer for the last nine years. Jane and her team tried to work with the hardware vendor in order to convince it to change the deal and to include CL. However, at this point, she does not believe that their efforts were successful.

Jane is concerned about the potential loss of a partnership with the hardware vendor that has been beneficial to both parties in the past. Obviously, she wants to restructure it to continue to be successful in the future. Jane is also concerned about the customer account team that will have to be repositioned or terminated as a result of this deal. This team includes people with tremendous knowledge of the company's products and services. Without a doubt, Jane prefers to retain all these people.

She defines her decision as "What is the best way to gain more business with the customer, provided that we can a) restructure the relationship with the hardware vendor in a win-win fashion and b) keep the account team?" Her decision map is shown in Figure 10-1.

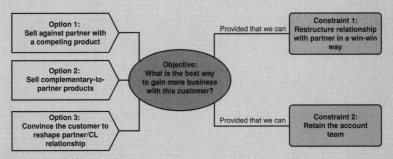

FIGURE 10-1

Jane's Original Decision Map

PART IV

While mapping her decision, Jane identifies three strategies of working with the customer:

Option 1: Offer customer products that compete with the hardware vendor.

Option 2: Offer customer products complementary to the hardware vendor.

Option 3: Convince the customer to reshape the deal to include CL in addition to the hardware vendor.

During the decision contemplation exercise, Jane realizes that her company made a mistake in allowing the hardware vendor to take the lead with the customer on this deal. This was the first time in the history of the company that they allowed another party to present their products for them. She realizes that this was rooted in fear that her company was smaller than the hardware vendor and would carry less clout with the powerful state agency. She also realized that, as a result of the other party's lead, certain strengths of her company's products and services were not even presented to the customer.

As this insight struck her, a new option started taking shape based on Options 2 and 3: "We can reshape the deal with the customer in a win-win-win way! And I just saw *how* we can do it! We should lead with a set of products and services that would be tremendously beneficial to the customer that the hardware vendor does not have in its product set. More importantly, we should do the bidding ourselves! All three parties—the customer, us, and the hardware vendor—will benefit, and *all* of my constraints will be satisfied!"

Jane defines the new option, Option 4, which becomes her clear choice. The new decision map is shown in Figure 10-2.

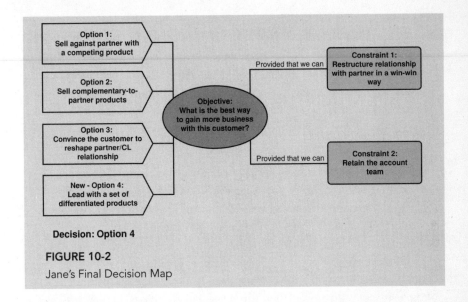

Decision: Option 4

FIGURE 10-2

Jane's Final Decision Map

What happened?

Jane found a different perspective—a shift from *looking up to* the partner because of its size to *being equal to or even stronger than* the partner from the perspective of additional product features valued by the customer.

Essentially, you can say that she is selecting a combination of Option 2 and Option 3, both of which were available to her before. But this new perspective allows her to add strength and power to Options 2 and 3 that were missing before. These options were "losers" if she approached them from the prior perspective—she did not know *how* to execute them. This new perspective allowed her to mentally take control. She immediately came up with a new option and an execution plan—a set of differentiated products to lead with that will allow her to accomplish Options 2 and 3.

Value 3: Clear Perspective Identifies a New Problem Area or Block

A new perspective illuminates a decision in a new light. In many cases, this new perspective enables us to clearly see the problem that was blocking us from making a decision. The path of action becomes clear. Consider the following example.

PART IV

EXAMPLE 10-4: STEVEN—IDENTIFYING A NEW SALES STRATEGY

Steven is the CEO of a company in the medical services sector that has had a tough year, in which sales declined 10 percent, morale is low, and the sales force "has lost the buzz." Steven is frustrated with the performance of his sales force. He is contemplating how to get the "buzz" back and get his company back on track.

During the exercise, he realizes that the market has changed over the last six months. As the market continues to change, the company as a whole has not supplied the sales force with the appropriate tools to deal with the changes. As the salespeople found it more difficult to close sales deals, morale declined: "Instead of helping them, the principals of the company, starting with me, became frustrated with the sales force, thus adding to the morale decline!" He also realized that they were not focused on getting market intelligence even though the two largest competitors are public.

What happened?

Steven's perspective shifted during the exercise, from blaming the sales force for not being effective in closing deals to realizing that the market shifted and that the sales team is continuing to sell with old tools. With a shift in perspective, a new problem area surfaced—senior management's responsibility for the current situation. An action plan became clear—"We need to work with the sales force and give them tools to win in the new environment."

Exercise

Take each of the framing factors you listed in the previous exercise, and look at the decision through that perspective. How does each perspective change your view? Write down your observations. You will be working with specific methods of changing perspectives in the next chapter.

Achieving Clarity of Perspective

I believe that arriving at solutions to difficult problems often requires one or both of the following: seeing the problem from a new perspective and making novel connections between two or more ideas.
Robin Hogarth[4]

Perspectives are similar to views of a document through a magnifying glass. Certain parts of the writing are visible; the rest is hidden from view. You move the magnifying glass, and it amplifies other aspects of the document.

Similarly, a fresh perspective can bring into view certain parts of the decision that were previously hidden, allowing you to see the right solution.

One of the most important skills in decision-making is to recognize when an issue requires a fresh perspective (needs to be reframed). Experienced decision makers warn that if you continually use an inappropriate frame—in other words, if you continue to simplify in ways that blind you to what is most significant about the problem—you will eventually cast yourself and your organization into deep problems[5]. The issue is that it is extremely difficult to recognize this moment, as the following example demonstrates.

EXAMPLE 10-5: KAREN—FUNDING A START-UP

Karen is the CEO of a start-up. She raised equity capital from a venture capital (VC) firm and built the company to the cash-neutral state but not yet to the profitability state. After five years, the VC that initially invested the money will start receiving "kickers" of 15 percent additional equity every year if the money is not repaid.

Karen has a strategy that will make the company grow faster, but this strategy requires a change in the company's business model. It will also require an additional investment to kick off the new business model. The VC is offering to take additional equity for this investment. The current negotiations focus on a package that is acceptable to both sides; the negotiations include Karen's deferred salary, equity positions of both parties, and other issues.

Details aside, in this deal, Karen will lose control of the company and may not even have the deferred salary repaid to her, not to mention returning her initial financial investment. Even though she believes in the new strategy, it is very risky. She also knows that it is possible that the new model may fail, and if so, she will not have any return on her five years of hard work, sacrifice, and financial investment.

Is Karen "framed?" Detailed issues are being discussed, yet it is unclear whether the company can be brought to a state that will enable Karen to financially gain at the level she initially intended. In fact, financial projections confirm that it will be incredibly difficult to reach that point. So, should the question be framed differently? "Knowing everything that I know about this business after five years, can this business deliver the financial return that I am looking for? If not, is this the time to consider exiting?"

If you ask Karen, she will deny that she is framed, as did all decision makers who were "framed" before the exercise and were actually able to reframe during the exercise. From the outsider's perspective, it may appear that Karen was framed. However, she was convinced that accepting the money even under bad conditions was the right path for her. She decided to proceed and is in the process of testing the new business model. The model seems to be working! Karen might have been right after all.

Good Practice for a Frame Artist
Before resolving a difficult issue, even if you believe that you are *not* framed, make it a practice to identify alternative frames and shift your perspective—ensuring that you are making the decision from the right perspective.
You often reach clarity by shifting your view of the problem until you find the one that clicks.

To be fair, decision makers realize that finding alternative perspectives is not easy. Many have devised their own methods of doing so.

One CEO gets involved in other people's decisions by sitting on boards of nonprofit organizations, where he gets a perspective of a completely different environment, which consists of greater struggles for money and more soul-touching and difficult problems, much different from his own. Even though this involvement does not necessarily help him in making his decisions, it provides a different view of his issues that, in his words, "has proven useful a number of times."

In order to reach clarity faster and more easily, learn to be a frame artist. Always assume that you are framed. Be able to generate alternative frames and shift your decision perspective a number of times until you find the right way to look at the decision.

Frame Artist's Process of Shifting Perspectives

To choose time is to save time.
Francis Bacon[6]

Each time you are facing a tough choice, go through the following process that summarizes techniques discussed in detail in the next chapter. It should not take you more than 15 minutes when you are used to it.

- Be in the Clarity State.
- Relax constraints.
- Stretch assumptions.
- Look for the crux of the issue.
- Stand back; find a broader viewpoint.
- Shift a loss into a gain.
- See the decision successfully implemented.

Most importantly, assume the "it's a game" attitude and have fun!

Key Point
The ability to reframe is a skill—the more you do it, the better you will be at it. Use every decision to practice. The ease of getting to decision clarity will follow.

CHAPTER 11

Becoming a Frame Artist—How to Master Clarity of Perspective

*Not he is great who can alter matter, but he who can alter [his]
state of mind.*
Ralph Waldo Emerson[1]

In order to reach clarity faster and easier, it is important to
learn to be a frame artist—routinely shift perspectives on a
decision before you make it. Always assume that you are
framed, and look for framing factors. Be able to easily generate alternative frames and shift your decision perspective a
number of times until you find the right way to look at the
decision.

This chapter covers six techniques that will help you generate new perspectives until you find a clear winner.

Technique 1: Constraints Relaxation

*The problem is that we attempt to solve the simplest questions
cleverly, thereby rendering them unusually complex. One should
seek the simple solution.*
Anton Chekhov[2]

Recognize that each constraint can provide a unique view of the decision, serving as a different magnifying glass. The constraint relaxation technique was developed from this observation.

For example, take Karen's case—Example 10-5 in the last chapter about negotiating with a VC on financing a start-up. Look at her decision through the constraint "Retain control over the company." In trying to satisfy this constraint, you will adjust your solutions accordingly, looking for an appropriate deal. Now look at her decision through a different constraint: "Ensure proper funding for testing the new business model." You will see a different set of issues from that view and will adjust your solutions accordingly.

Process of Constraints Relaxation

The technique consists of the following steps that have to be done *for each constraint* that you listed during the process of constraints clarification:

1. **Get into the Clarity State.**

2. **Determine the importance of the constraint.** Ask yourself: "How important is this constraint?"

   I am not talking about force-ranking constraints, rather just noticing a constraint's importance to you in the overall scope of things. I've often found that when a constraint is seriously contemplated, the decision maker adjusts its importance. You might realize that the constraint is not as important as it seemed. I've often heard: "The perceived importance came from my being emotional about it. When I was able to detach, I realized that the constraint was not nearly as important as I thought."

   Or, on the contrary, you might add a constraint as almost an afterthought during the creation of the decision map. Then you realize that this is the most critical constraint to consider.

3. **Relax the constraint to a point where you can remove it from consideration.**

   A lot of times, your rational being will resist the action of removing a constraint—"This is very important; I cannot take it away!" It is worth a try, however, to imagine a situation in which this constraint does not exist. How would the situation change?

What would need to happen to allow this constraint to be taken away? How would it shift your perspective on the whole decision? And would it? Which option would you choose if you did not have this constraint? Which one fits the situation best without this constraint?

4. **Maximize the constraint as if it is the only one affecting your decision.**

   The easiest way to accomplish such maximization is to add the constraint to the objective and focus on the resulting expanded objective to the exclusion of everything else. How does it change your view of the whole situation related to the decision? If this is the main objective, what would you do? Does this view offer new solutions? Are they captured in the options? Which option addresses it best?

5. **Identify ways to address the constraint through actions unrelated to your decision.**

   Can you see any actions that can be taken now that will take this constraint out of consideration for this decision or diminish its importance? Actions unrelated to a decision can often eliminate a constraint. By leaving unnecessary constraints in the decision definition, you limit your solutions without the need to do so.

Let's demonstrate the power of this technique on Bruce's decision.

EXAMPLE 11-1: BRUCE—SELECTING FINANCING FOR A START-UP

Bruce is an experienced CEO. This company is his third start-up. Less than a year ago, Bruce sold his previous company and was fortunate to receive a significant multiple on his investment of time, money, and energy over the last seven years. For this new venture, Bruce has teamed up with two people who have demonstrated a "proof of concept" for a new product. He became excited about growing the company from this base through franchising.

He is faced with a financing decision for his new venture. He has several good options, but none address his and his partners' needs fully:

- Option 1: Bootstrap the company utilizing his own and his partners' money.

- Option 2: Accept investment from a private equity fund. The problem with this option is that the money is offered at a lower valuation than he would have liked.

- Option 3: Continue to search for investors with the right valuation.

- Option 4: Find a strategic partner. Bruce has started talking to several potential partners and sees a growing interest.

Bruce listed several concerns related to his decision and converted them to constraints:

Concern:	Constraint:
1. He and his team wanted to open the first facility in three months.	1. Open the first facility in three months.
2. Even though he was unaware of direct competition, he wanted to proceed quickly and benefit from being first to market and the associated publicity wave.	2. Get the benefits of a publicity wave.
3. He was concerned about losing momentum. If the founders continued to look for money and not sign the lease for the first facility, they might lose the space that was offered at a good rate. They might lose vendors that have been lined up for the grand opening of the facility, not to mention losing the team's excited "drive" to get the company going.	3. Keep the momentum going.
4. The aspect of valuing the business at the right level was especially important to Bruce.	4. Ensure fair valuation.

Concern:	Constraint:
5. His partner, was more concerned about having enough money to make the venture a long-term success and was scared of running out of money before the concept could be demonstrated.	5. Ensure having enough money.

The decision map of Bruce's decision is presented in Figure 11-1.

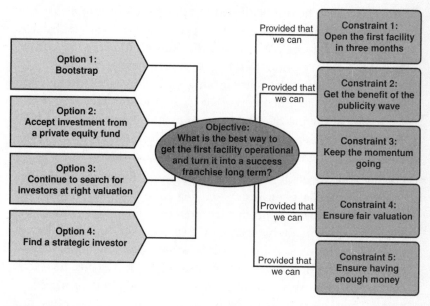

FIGURE 11-1

Bruce's Decision Map

As Bruce considers each constraint through the constraint relaxation exercise, several things become clear:

- As he considers the requirement to open the new facility in three months (constraint 1), he realizes that it is not important whether the first facility is opened in three, four, or even six months. What is important is keeping the momentum going with the team and laying the groundwork for not only the first facility but also for the whole franchise. Thus, constraint 1 is captured in constraint 3, so constraint 1 can be eliminated.

- Getting the benefit of the publicity wave (constraint 2) would be nice, but it's really not important for this decision at all. Constraint 2 can also be eliminated.

- Keeping the momentum going (constraint 3) is critical! As Bruce contemplates it, he gets the feeling that this is the most critical constraint for the decision. From this viewpoint, accepting money from the fund (Option 2) is the only viable option.

- Ensuring fair valuation (constraint 4) is enormously important. However, when he forces himself to take this constraint away from consideration, he breaths a sigh of relief that there are no obstacles to choosing Option 2. When he forces himself to make this constraint the only constraint on his decision, a new perspective emerges. Fair valuation is important, but having gone through two start-ups previously, he knows that fairly priced money is only a small part of the puzzle. There are many hurdles to overcome before his dream becomes a reality. His conclusion—"Take the money *now*, even though it might be slightly more expensive."

- Having gone through two previous start-ups, Bruce knows the importance of the last constraint—having enough money. His partner is particularly insistent on this requirement, having spent his career as an executive in a large company. Bruce knows, however, that there are methods to control cash flow and spend money slowly—ensuring that a little bit of money goes a long way. Thus, he is less concerned about this constraint than his partner. In the process of maximizing this constraint, he realizes that Option 2 provides covenants for raising additional money later when the venture is more established. Besides, if everything goes well, they can get the money at better valuation.

The constraint relaxation exercise helps Bruce identify the most important constraint as well as two less important but critical ones. Different perspectives on the decision that are created during the exercise suggest that the second option is the most viable option. Moreover, he sees a way to negotiate the deal such that additional money is available to the company later and at a higher valuation.

Every decision maker is essentially a visualizer and an actualizer. As you visualize something, you see exactly how to make it happen. The constraint relaxation process gives a specific method to do it effectively.

Exercise

Review the decision map created earlier of the situation you chose in Chapter 1, "The Key to Mastering Decisions." Contemplate your decision constraints in the Clarity State according to the process outlined previously. In preparation, record the steps of the technique on a tape recorder, leaving some time between the steps, and play them back as you consider the constraints, one after another. Alternatively, ask someone to read the steps to you.

Write down your observations.

Technique 2: Assumption Stretching

Never assume.
Anonymous

This technique is similar to the constraints relaxation exercise, but instead of constraints as your magnifying glass, you look at the decision from the perspective of each assumption.

Process for Clarifying Assumptions

Go through the following steps for each assumption:

1. Get into the Clarity State.
2. Take an assumption away from consideration. Does it change your view of the situation? How? Which option would you choose if you did not have this assumption? Which one best fits the situation without this assumption?
3. Ask yourself "What would need to change in the environment for the assumption to be wrong?" Check each potential environmental change against reality. Have you recently confirmed that there is no new information about this potential change?
4. Maximize the assumption as if it is the only one affecting your decision.

In Example 10-5 in the previous chapter, in which Karen was negotiating with a VC about funding a start-up, she had an implicit assumption: "I am continuing with this start-up no matter what!" If she went through the process in this section, the step of removing this assumption from consideration (step 2) would have opened her thinking to other options—exiting, for example.

Let's take Brian's example, Example 10-1 in the previous chapter, about selecting a vendor. The implicit assumption is "The current vendor does not negotiate." Looking for "What would make this assumption wrong" (step 3) would have been fruitful in this case. You can come up with a number of reasons why the current vendor might change its negotiating position. It may be a weakened financial situation, a change in management, a stronger competitive product, and so on. Consciously checking these factors for validity could have provided a good set of ideas for a potential negotiation, not to mention that it would have identified the news item about the CEO of the current vendor retiring.

Good Practice for a Frame Buster
Always check your assumptions for validity.
The process of assumption clarification identifies perceived or false constraints and opens your decision to creative solutions.

Exercise
Contemplate your decision assumptions in the Clarity State according to the process outlined in this section. Write down your observations.

Technique 3: Identifying the Crux of the Issue

Definition
The crux of a decision is the most important, critical parameter among all parameters related to a decision.

The crux provides an "angle" from which to look at the situation so that the solution becomes clear. Identifying the crux of the issue is simplifying at the extreme—find one parameter, and ... you have clarity. Not all decisions can be resolved like this, but when they can be, you should take advantage of this technique.

In Stuart's example, Example 10-2 in the previous chapter, of completing the construction of two new plants, the constraint "Deliver consistent product quality" served as the "crux" for making the decision.

Sometimes one of the constraints stands out as the most critical issue, as in Stuart's case. Other times, the crux is not even on the decision map, but is triggered by the contemplation of one of the constraints, as the following example demonstrates.

EXAMPLE 11-2: JOEL—EVALUATING AN ACQUISITION

Joel is President and CEO of a multibillion-dollar division of a very large conglomerate company, one of the largest in the world (let's call it LG). Joel was called by the Chairman of the company on Friday afternoon and told about a phone call that the Chairman received from a member of the board of a very large computer company (we will call it CMP) earlier that week. The director wanted to know whether LG would be interested in acquiring CMP. An LG board meeting was scheduled for Tuesday of next week, where the Chairman wanted to discuss this situation and make a decision. Joel's division was a natural fit for the proposed acquisition within LG. The Chairman wanted Joel and his team to work through the weekend and prepare a "pros and cons" presentation as well as a recommendation by Monday morning.

Even though Joel's division was considered to be a beneficiary of the potential acquisition, CMP had little overlap with Joel's business. As Joel's team was pulling together information about the acquisition candidate, issues facing CMP started emerging. A new technology platform was putting pressure on CMP's revenue and margins numbers. Regardless, the company was still the leader in its field.

On the other hand, LG was feeling "invincible," having successfully done a series of acquisitions and having beaten analysts' projections on growth year after year.

The decision was difficult because Joel personally felt that this acquisition would be a great entry into a growing technology market that LG has not played in before. He and his team were excited about additional value that the acquisition could bring to other divisions across LG. However, he believed that LG in general, and his division in particular, did not know much about CMP's market and business model.

Joel's decision map is shown in Figure 11-2.

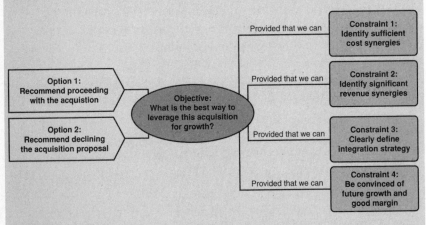

FIGURE 11-2
Joel's Decision Map

Late on Sunday night, Joel realized that his time for making the decision was up. He decided to recommend passing on the acquisition (Option 2) to the Chairman on Monday morning.

What happened?

Joel's team worked hard to collect data and put together a convincing story addressing the objective and constraints as presented in Figure 11-2. Joel was convinced that even though the entry into the computer arena would be of interest to his division and to LG in general, it was not the main objective behind the acquisition. The main objective was the growth acceleration factor. If the acquisition could give his division and LG in general a boost in growth, it was worth doing.

As Joel contemplated factors involved in the acquisition and the projections that were put together, the crux of the matter struck him. He realized that one question was critical to deciding this issue, and it had to do with the market situation that CMP found itself in. In order to maintain and potentially accelerate its leadership position, CMP would need to rebuild itself and address the new technology platform threat. The critical question for LG then became "What do we know that they do not know that will allow us to solve their strategic problem better? What would our plan be?"

As you can see, the crux was not on the decision map. It was most likely triggered by constraint 4—be convinced of future growth and good margins. Joel realized that he could not offer a solution to CMP that would convince him that this constraint could be satisfied. This was probably the point at which the crux question formulated in his mind.

The decision became clear in that instant. Nobody at LG, including Joel, had a good answer to the crux question. He became absolutely certain that LG should decline the acquisition and was able to convincingly argue this point at the board meeting.

The "crux" is usually hidden from view, crowded out by other important concerns involved in the decision. Going through the constraints relaxation and assumptions-stretching technique first provides a good base for identifying the "crux." Working with constraints in this manner "shakes up" the current frame, identifies different points of view on a decision, and in many cases triggers the understanding of the crux.

Process for Crux Identification

- Get into the Clarity State.
- Go through the constraints relaxation and assumption-stretching exercise.
- Ask yourself: "Having considered all the constraints, what is the one question I should ask that is most critical for this problem? What's the crux of the issue?"

> **Exercise**
>
> Do you have a most critical question behind your decision? What is it?

Technique 4: Expanding Your View

Our life is frittered away by detail... Simplify, simplify.
Henry David Thoreau[3]

Achieving clarity often involves stepping back and seeing the decision set in a larger context with a longer time span[4,5]. The broader your perspective, the clearer you can be about your decision. Again, the question is *how*.

One executive told me that he loves learning about astronomy and the stars. The slow evolution of the planets, stars, and constellations fascinates him and, interestingly, provides a different perspective on his difficult decisions. "When I face a particularly trying decision, and for me difficult decisions are mostly related to people, I force myself to become a planet or a star and imagine myself traveling through space and time. Then, when I look at my decision from that perspective, my life looks miniscule, not to mention my problem, which seems really tiny and unimportant."

If you are not into astronomy, use one of the following two techniques in order to obtain a longer time frame and a bigger perspective.

Process of "Stepping Back"

- Get into the Clarity State.
- Create a vision of your business, and imagine yourself and your business five or, even better, 10 years in the future. Try to create active scenes for this future with yourself being an active participant in these scenes. Involve as many senses as possible. From that perspective, look at the current decision. Do you see any options that you are not considering? Do you see any shifts in importance?

- Take an even larger view—your overall life's perspective. Your whole life is in front of you as a series of major events condensed to fit on one piece of paper, including your past achievements and all the plans you have for the future. Now, look at the current decision—how important is it? Any advice you can give yourself? Do you see any shifts in importance?

Peak performers use the skill of mental rehearsal or visualization. They mentally run through important events before they happen. By doing so, they often identify factors that are important for "winning" and that they should pay closer attention to.

Many decisions require detailed and intense computations and projections. It is easy to get "framed" by these details. Forcing yourself to take a longer view is a necessary step to detach from these details. Consider the following example.

EXAMPLE 11-3: PATRICK—SATISFYING FUTURE POWER REQUIREMENTS

Patrick is the CEO of a company that delivers power to states in its jurisdiction. The power distribution is governed by a set of cooperatives—an organization with a complex structure that he also runs. His company delivers that power for the cooperatives to the states. Patrick is wrestling with the issue of how to satisfy the next generation of power needs. In three years, his company will need to provide 150 additional units of power.

One of the difficulties of this situation is that 150 power units is not a lot of energy. The company's model is to control its generation assets. But acquiring a full coal asset or a full gas asset is not necessary to generate this additional amount of energy. If the company were to buy assets, it would end up as a minority holder, or part of the asset would not get used. The company is also concerned about gas prices going up over time and thus increasing energy prices for its customers.

Patrick is considering several options:

- Option 1: Buy part of a distressed gas asset (a number of them are on the market).

PART IV

- Option 2: Buy part of the coal asset (very limited supply). The one coal asset that they have found will require additional investment because of the need to address certain environmental concerns. This asset is also old, and because the company will be in a minority position, it might not be able to ensure performance stability.

- Option 3: Add a fourth coal unit to the existing coal plant.

- Option 4: Obtain power contracts to satisfy additional energy needs.

Patrick's decision map is presented in Figure 11-3.

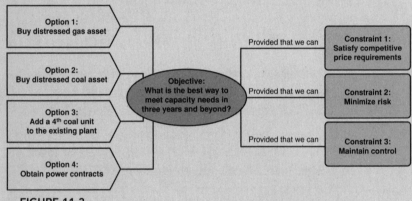

FIGURE 11-3

Patrick's Decision Map

Patrick decides to add the fourth coal unit to the existing plant (Option 3) and to obtain a short-term contract before this unit becomes operational (Option 4). Before the exercise, Option 3 was the most undesirable option.

What happened?

Patrick's insights came from taking a longer view on the decision overall, while going through the constraint relaxation exercise and contemplating constraint 3 (a way to maintain control). From the perspective of maintaining control over the power generation resources, adding the fourth unit to the existing plant (Option 3) is the best option. The timing of this addition is totally in his company's hands. Moreover, the plant's operation is being outsourced to a large power company that can be expected to participate in the funding of the unit. Together, they can maintain control over the asset.

Previously, adding the fourth coal unit to the existing power plant was not a desirable option because of its high investment and the fact that the company did not see a way to utilize all of its capacity. However, by looking at the utilization over a longer time frame, it became clear that over time, the company could ramp up and utilize the whole capacity. A new option crystallized—find the right time to install the fourth coal unit, and supplement the needs by obtaining power contracts in the meantime.

> **Exercise**
>
> Put your decision into a broader context with a longer time frame. Be creative. Visualize as many parts of your future environment as possible five or 10 years in the future. Replay it in your mind several times until you are satisfied.
>
> Now imagine that you are describing this decision from that future point. What do you say? What factors would you stress? What factors are visible from the future that are not visible today?

Technique 5: Shifting a Loss Problem Statement into Gain

The greatest deception men suffer is from their own opinions.
Leonardo Da Vinci[6]

Negative emergency situations project strong frames on decision makers. When you are in crisis mode, you barely have time to think. You react. Situations with solutions that have negative outcomes also project strong negative frames. In such situations, the difficulty of a decision is intensified due to its formulation. Actively shifting the negative frame into a positive one produces a perspective shift that can open additional options, as the following example demonstrates.

PART IV

EXAMPLE 11-4: MAT—SURVIVING A COUNTRY'S ECONOMIC CRISIS

Mat has been with a manufacturing company located in Turkey for the last 14 years and was promoted from project manager to general manager. Several years ago, he became the CEO of the company.

Two years after becoming the CEO and growing the business to become one of the top three vendors in his market, Mat found himself in the midst of the country's economic crisis. In one month, the currency was devalued 30% overnight, and a month later, there was another 40–50% decrease. It became clear then that the situation was irreversible and had to be addressed.

The difficulty was that all options on the table were not good choices from the business point of view:

- Option 1: Reduce prices and sell products at a loss, but keep the market share.

- Option 2: Keep prices flat or even raise them, but suffer a revenue drop.

- Option 3: Utilize Turkey's manufacturing capacity and export products to the neighboring countries, and manage costs by closing offices, but maintain revenue. The company had ventured into the neighboring countries in the past but was unsuccessful due to fierce competition with local manufacturers.

Obviously, all these options required layoffs and the need to face a further decrease in the company's morale in the midst of Turkey's already-tough economic environment.

In addition to the fact that this is a complex and unfortunate situation, the decision is more difficult due to the formulation of the problem. Mat's main responsibility as CEO is to profitably grow the company. In this emergency situation, this objective cannot be satisfied.

By the nature of the setup, his objective is formulated as a loss statement: minimize damage to the company. His constraints are also loss minimization statements: minimize the layoffs, minimize the loss of manufacturing capabilities, and minimize the cash drain.

Research has shown that response to loss is more extreme than response to gain[7]. According to prospect theory, decision makers tend to avoid risk concerning gains and seek risk concerning losses. The theory suggests that most individuals will choose a $10,000 sure gain over a 50 percent chance of gaining $20,000 because the utility placed on $20,000 under the circumstances is not twice as great as the value placed on $10,000. However, most individuals will choose a 50 percent chance of a $20,000 loss over a sure loss of $10,000 because the negative value placed on $20,000 under the circumstances is not twice as great as the negative value placed on $10,000.

This well-known phenomenon makes Mat's choice even more difficult.

Mat's initial decision map appears in Figure 11-4. Mat phrased his objective as "What is the best way to minimize the impact of the current economic environment on the company?" As he was contemplating the decision, he realized that the crux of the issue is how to take the company through this downturn and help it survive. He decided that he should focus on the long-term sustainability of the business.

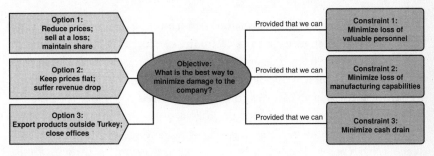

FIGURE 11-4

Mat's Decision Map

He reworded his objective as "What is the best way to ensure sustainability and long-term accelerated growth?" This new formulation puts a completely different perspective on the issue and opens new opportunities to be included as solutions. Namely, the company can focus on streamlining its processes and developing new products during the downturn. In the upturn, these efforts have a high chance of strengthening the company's market position and enabling faster growth. Mat's changed decision map appears in Figure 11-5.

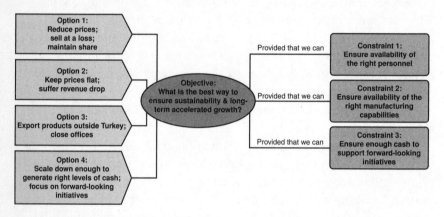

FIGURE 11-5
Mat's Decision Formulated as a Gain

As you can see, the new decision definition has different constraints. Now, Mat has to ensure that the company executes sufficient layoffs in order to generate enough cash from operations to sustain the business and support the forward-looking initiatives during the downturn. In preparation for the layoff, the company will need to ensure that the right personnel are available for the forward-looking initiatives.

This is a simple technique that follows the adage of "think positively." However, in the midst of a crisis situation, this is difficult to do. Contemplating such a decision in the Clarity State helps to enable this shift.

Exercise

Is your decision formulated as a loss statement? If so, redo it using the technique from this section.

Recollect another decision that was set in a negative context. Rework it into a positive statement. How different would your actions have been if you had formulated it this way initially?

Technique 6: Looking at Your Decision from the Perspective of a Realized Objective in the Future

A man to carry on a successful business must have imagination. He must see things as in a vision, a dream of the whole thing.
Charles M. Schwab[8]

Great inventors develop their inventions starting from the end point. They see it done. They play with it in their mind's lab until all parts of the invention are perfect.

Key Point
Effective executives know that looking at the situation from a success point in the future—when the current issue is successfully addressed—can create new ideas for its implementation.

The process is very simple and involves these steps:

- Be in the Clarity State with its feeling of excitement and self-power. The emotional side is critically important for this exercise.

- Create a picture, a scene in your mind that symbolizes a resolution of the situation related to this decision, a realization of the objective and the constraints to the fullest. Use as many senses as possible in this picture. Create a feeling of positive momentum! Be there and live it! Fully get into the feeling of "We've done it!" You might see yourself talking to a friend or business associate and describing *how easy it was* to get to this objective and resolve this situation.

PART IV

- From this perspective of the realized objective in the future, ask yourself what is the best way to get here. What is the easiest path, the most fun for you? Is there another way to look at the whole situation and get there faster and easier? Is there another option that you are not considering?

  It's like you are standing on top of the mountain and looking at all the paths to get there, but knowing that only one path represents the best route for you. What is it?

The following is an example of how this process resulted in the creation of a new product.

EXAMPLE 11-5: RICHARD—A NEW PRODUCT IDEA

Richard is the founder and CEO of a large software company. The company went public several years ago and is doing "extremely well."

Just recently, in order to simplify product development and maintenance, the company integrated databases from two separate product lines. One product line was introduced to the market 10 years ago and was considered within the company to be a "cash cow." However, the demand for this product is slowing down. Another product line is relatively new; it was introduced to the market five years ago. It has a high price tag due to its built-in sophisticated computations and broad, sometimes esoteric, functionality. The latter product line has never caught up in the market.

Richard asked his VP of development to consider rationalization options that the company should consider implementing in the future. He just attended a presentation on this topic by the product development team. The team proposed a number of rationalization paths and recommended pursuing all of them in a gradual manner with a target to complete the rationalization by year's end. Richard's decision map is shown in Figure 11-6.

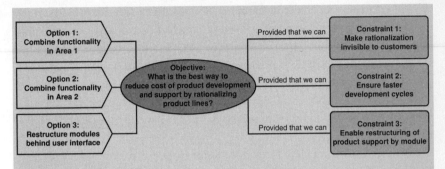

FIGURE 11-6

Richard's Decision Map

In reviewing the proposed solutions and the recommendation of the team, Richard develops the concept of a new product line! The new product is primarily based on the second product line, but it is "light"—with complexities of the second product line eliminated, and with added capabilities from the first "cash cow" line.

The idea came to him in a flash, and he was totally convinced that the company should act on this idea.

What happened?

Richard told me that as I introduced the analogy of standing on the mountaintop, he literally imagined himself on the top of the mountain, because he was an avid hiker. He imagined a situation when product rationalization would be complete and the company would be able to streamline product development and support as a result. He became incredibly excited about this outcome.

As he was standing on this mountaintop, it occurred to him to look at the paths leading to the top—one very steep, one thorny, and one very steady but extremely long. Associations between proposed product rationalization options and the paths formed themselves, he said. And then he saw a perfect path that was easy, straight, and in the shade. He said that it was like a lightning bolt—he had an idea for a new product!

PART IV

He is convinced that the fact that he looked at solutions from the success point in the future was fundamental to this insight. He was assuming that a certain amount of rationalization had been accomplished by that time. It enabled him to see a unique combination of functionality that otherwise, he claims, he would not have been able to spot. He was also excited about the fact that this idea was easy to implement because many of the changes required were done in the database integration between the two product lines.

It was interesting that his whole team opposed him when he shared his idea. They cited many reasons why the company should not do it, including cannibalization of other product lines, a need for extra support resources, limited product capabilities in this new product, and low market response, among others. Richard spent time convincing the team and persisted in acting on his idea.

The story ends well. Within two months of his insight, the company introduced a new product that is having great success in the marketplace. It pays to picture yourself vividly as winning. This alone will contribute immeasurably to your success.

Exercise

In the Clarity State, imagine a success point in the future when your decision is fully implemented. Use your mind as a lab to create this success point. Be there and live it! When you feel that you are totally engrossed in the future, look back at the present decision. What are the implementation paths that you have not considered before that can lead to this success point?

Frame Artist's Toolbox

Each time you are facing a tough choice, go through the following techniques discussed in this chapter—this is your toolbox to identify additional frames and shift perspectives.

- Be in the Clarity State.
- Relax constraints.
- Stretch assumptions.

- Look for the crux of the issue.
- Stand back; find a broader viewpoint.
- Shift a loss into a gain.
- See the decision successfully implemented.

Create your own methods using visualization and imagination. Most importantly, practice! Remember, practice makes perfect.

CHAPTER 12

Bull's-eye!—How to Align with the Right Outcome

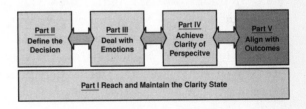

The understanding that underlies the right decision grows out of the clash and conflict of divergent opinions and out of the serious consideration of competing alternatives.
Peter F. Drucker[1]

A decision is a risk-taking judgment. In addition to selecting an alternative, the critical component of this judgment is a prediction of how the future will unfold based on the current knowledge. I call it vision power. Effective leaders are highly skilled in vision power.

By making a decision and selecting an alternative from a set of options, you announce to the world your vision for the future. You might be the only person with this vision. And it might be wrong. Taking this stance requires courage. The higher the level of irreversibility of a decision, the more courage it requires.

Key Point
Visionary leaders are willing to commit to their image of the future and take the risk that comes with it.

Taking this stance requires a definite internal alignment—a true belief that you are making a right choice—a choice that is right for you and the business. Without this true belief in the rightness of the choice, it is hard to summon the courage to proceed with it.

This part of the Clarity State Decision-Making process is a culmination of all prior work with your decision. Having gone through defining your definite aim—a decision complete with the objective, constraints, and success factors, balancing your emotions and reframing—this is the final step to establish clarity. You are ready to hit the target—your aim is clear, and you are fully prepared to make the final choice.

Key Point
Clarity comes from exercising your vision power on each solution alternative—projecting it into the future—and then assessing the results for the best fit with your decision aim.
Clarity State is your platform. Imagination is your tool. Emotions are your guides.

The critical parameter of vision power is the ability to perceive *the most likely course* of future developments. Exercising your vision power gives you other benefits as well. You can identify critical milestones, anticipate potential environmental changes, identify barriers to success, and anticipate them. The basis for this predictive judgment is largely intuitive. Vision power sharpens with practice and continuous assessment of the past decisions' results.

Exercise

What is your vision power? Recollect three to five important decisions you've made over the last three years. Pick the ones with apparent results that can be assessed now.

How close was your future prediction to what happened in reality? Did you make any changes to your original plan in the course of the implementation? How many did you anticipate?

Did you have any unexpected turns or surprises during the implementation? Could you have anticipated them?

You can develop your vision power by learning to educate your intuition and engage imagination in your decision-making. You must first clearly see a thing in your mind before you can do it.

Most of us use one or two analytical methods to evaluate decision options—thus educating our intuition. The approach I used to enable this intuitive sense to get you to clarity is imagination and visualization. I asked decision makers to use their minds in the Clarity State as a playground for their ideas—considering solution options from various angles, identifying reasons for failure, and evaluating key uncertainties.

Before we discuss the techniques of solution sensitivity analysis and solution alignment that capture this approach, let's briefly overview methods that we commonly use to educate intuition.

Educating Intuition—A Brief Overview

Doubt and mistrust are the mere panic of timid imagination, which the steadfast heart will conquer, and the large mind transcend.
Helen Keller[2]

Executives are known to use vision power in the following situations[3]:

- Where there is a high level of uncertainty.
- Where there is little previous precedent.
- Where variables are less scientifically predictable.
- Where facts are limited.

- Where facts do not clearly indicate the direction to take.
- When analytical data is of little use (such as if new trends are emerging).
- Where there are several plausible alternative solutions to choose from, with good arguments for each.
- Where time is limited and there is pressure to be right.
- For negotiations and personnel decisions.

Most strategic business decisions qualify under one or more of these categories and thus require the use of intuition and vision power. Consider the following example, where Paul's time to decide is limited, there is pressure to be right, market recovery from a downturn is uncertain, and the analytical data is of little use.

EXAMPLE 12-1: PAUL—WHEN ALL CHOICES ARE "BAD"

Paul is the CEO of a telecommunications company. A part of his company's operations is under government regulations. A year and a half ago, his company decided that it needed to expand its reach into a certain area and proceeded to obtain government approval for such an expansion. As the process dragged on, competition in the market intensified. Previously, the company could have raised prices to cover the cost of the investment. Under current circumstances, this is much harder to do.

On the other hand, the company just completed a full review of its "plant" from the service reliability point of view. One of the recommendations is to make this investment, but for service reliability purposes. The cost is estimated to be approximately $100 million.

The regulation allowing the company to proceed with the investment has just been issued. However, the timing is bad—Paul's industry is in the middle of a slump with a slow recovery, as Paul sees it. The company is facing another layoff. However, the regulation has a time limit within which the company has to act on this issue.

As Paul sees it, he has only two options:

- Option 1: Make the investment now.

- Option 2: Negotiate with the government to prolong the time frame for making the investment. Delay the investment until the market recovers.

Neither option is good. Making an investment now, as the company is about to do another layoff, does not make sense to Paul. Delaying the investment raises service reliability issues.

In such tough situations, we commonly use methods such as evaluating pros and cons, building probability trees, eliminating alternatives, evaluating options relative to a reference point, and making trade-offs. It is well recognized by scientists that any analytical method creates more questions than it answers. As a result, analytical methods usually do not indicate a clear choice. However, realize that these methods of evaluating alternatives *feed your intuition* with data and analysis and are critically important as stepping-stones to clarity.

Key Point
Make sure that your intuition is fed with as much data and analysis as possible.

Here is a brief overview of methods commonly used, as mentioned by decision makers during my interviews with them.

Assignment

As you go through the following descriptions of the analytical methods, apply them to your decision. Make notes. Assess the level of clarity that you gain with the application of each method.

If you use other analytical methods that are not listed here, apply them to your decision. The objective of the exercise is to have as much information about each alternative as you can before you make your final decision at the end of the chapter.

PART V

Method #1: Evaluating Pros and Cons

Evaluating pros and cons is a simple method of evaluating positive and negative factors for each solution alternative and selecting the alternative with the most positive factors[4]. Almost everyone agrees that this technique is useful, but sometimes it is more confusing than helpful, especially if more than a handful of alternatives is involved.

I heard a story of a CEO who was flying to Europe from the United States to complete a business transaction. All parameters of the deal were already negotiated, and his task was to sign it and go through the celebratory ceremonies. His problem was that he was not sure that he should sign it. His team was convinced that this was a "great" deal for the company, but he was not. He told me that something (a parameter, maybe) was escaping him and had been escaping him while the due diligence and the evaluation of the deal were going on. On the way to Europe, he found himself writing page after page of pros and cons. However, he failed to find this parameter during the flight.

He signed the deal. However, looking at it from the current vantage point, his advice is "When not clear, do not go forward." Realistically, though, could he have not signed it? Probably not.

Method #2: Eliminating Alternatives

This method involves "circling" through alternatives, continuously looking for ways to eliminate them as options, thus reducing the number of choices and arriving at a final selection. When people are confronted with complex choices among a number of alternatives, they typically use what researchers call "noncompensatory" strategies that allow no trade-offs[5] and provide a method to gradually eliminate choices until only one choice remains. The following are a couple of examples of such strategies:

a. Eliminating alternatives outside a certain predefined solution boundary that is considered acceptable (a "conjunctive strategy"). For example, if you are looking for a certain level of business growth as one of your decision success factors, you will eliminate alternatives that do not deliver the minimum desired level of growth.

b. Choosing the most important dimension for comparison and the most desirable alternative based on this dimension (a "lexicographic strategy"). If more than one alternative remains, the decision maker takes the next important dimension and does the comparison, and so on, until only one alternative remains.

You can use this strategy by first selecting your decision objective as the most critical dimension. Select the alternatives that would satisfy your objective. You are likely to have more than one alternative remaining. Select the most important constraint as the next dimension, and eliminate alternatives that do not satisfy this dimension. Proceed by selecting the next most important constraint until you are left with one alternative.

Listen to your own feedback as you are doing this exercise. You might feel resistance when you are asked to select the most important constraint, for example. It is because you might have several constraints at the same level of importance that you would like to be addressed in the solution. However, doing this exercise will feed your intuition with what is most important to you in this decision and what factors you are not willing to compromise on.

c. Assigning weights to all parameters related to your decision and combining these weights with probabilities that estimate how well each parameter will be satisfied in each alternative (an "elimination-by-aspects strategy").

This strategy is a more complex variation of the lexicographic strategy. It can be useful if you have many constraints and all of them are at a similarly high level of importance. For example, you can decide to assign weights from 1 to 5, with 5 being high. You are likely to rate your objective as 5 and then proceed to rate constraints. For each alternative, evaluate the level of how well this parameter will be satisfied by this alternative, and assign a probability. Then multiply this probability by the weight of this parameter. Then calculate the sum of all parameter evaluations for each alternative. At the end of this process, each alternative will have one number associated with it. In this strategy, the alternative with the highest number is selected.

All these strategies are imperfect and are unlikely to lead you to clarity. However, selecting one of them and applying it to your decision will give you valuable information. For example, it often happens that when an analytical method leads you to a particular alternative, you realize that this alternative is not right for your business.

Method #3: Evaluating Options Relative to a Reference Point

Subconsciously, we all employ this method of evaluating solutions relative to a reference point, usually comparing all options to a status quo situation as a reference point. In some cases, decision makers compare the quality of their decision to what might have happened if they had made a different choice. The comparison of imaginary outcomes is sometimes referred to as "counterfactual reasoning" because it relies on hypothetical events[6]. It forms a basis for regret theory. One executive mentioned to me that this is exactly how he makes choices when everything else fails: he assigns the amount of regret to each choice—the amount he will experience if he does not go with a particular alternative. And then he selects the alternative that has the least amount of regret associated with it.

When you are comparing options with a defined reference point, researchers call such a reference point an "anchor." Selecting a good anchor is critical for this technique because it has been proven that *we rarely deviate from an established anchor*. Negotiators know this fact. When they first propose a price in negotiations, they are looking to establish an anchor.

Because you will subconsciously use this method anyway, it is a good practice to know the anchor that you are using and how relevant it is to your decision. For example, one manager characterized the current environment in his company as a "total mess." His decision was intended to completely change the situation. However, by comparing alternatives to the current situation—his reference point—he was reacting positively to solutions that proposed incremental rather than radical changes that he was looking for. He made a conscious effort to change the anchor—compare alternatives to a situation that his competitor was in—thus "raising the bar" for his options. If your anchor is the current situation, but it is not a good reference point, make a conscious effort to select a better anchor.

Method #4: Building Probability Trees

Many decision makers employ probability trees in evaluating a situation with a number of complex choices and major uncertainties involved in each choice[7]. These diagrams are a useful way to organize information about the joint and conditional probabilities of various combinations of events.

The major benefit of creating a probability tree is that you have to consciously think through the following questions for each alternative:

- What are the key uncertainties?
- What are the possible outcomes of these uncertainties?
- What are the chances of occurrence of each possible outcome?
- What are the consequences of each outcome?

The process involves building a tree for each alternative that has key uncertainties as nodes and possible outcomes of these uncertainties as branches. Each branch is assigned a probability, making sure that the total number at each node is 100%. When you are done, you can compile a probability of any outcome that you are interested in by multiplying the probabilities of branches leading to this outcome in the tree. You can also add expected monetary value to your tree. The expected monetary value of an outcome is the probability of this event multiplied by the monetary value of this outcome.

Even though the creation of probability trees is a useful method, researchers have proven that humans are inherently bad at assigning probabilities to future events[8]. Our estimates of probabilities and of the desirability of consequences can be influenced by such factors as framing, grouping, representative thinking, and the ease of memory recall[9].

Also recognize that projections into the future will differ from person to person because they are based on individual experience. As a result, different ways of making such projections can actually make people disagree on potential outcomes and thus on the solution selection.

Disregarding the negatives, building a probability tree can serve as a good tool for "educating intuition." As you go through the choices, you balance the estimated probabilities of possible consequences with the desirability of such consequences and intuitively evaluate choices from both perspectives. The selection is then made based on highest desirability and probability.

PART V

If you tried to estimate the probability of an event without creating a probability tree, you might become a victim of what researchers call "scenario estimating[9]." Most people fall into a "compound probability fallacy," which simply means that if the probability of the final event consists of the probabilities of several events leading to the final event, most people will tend to overestimate the final probability.

From a mathematics perspective, this is obvious. The probability of the final event is a multiple of probabilities of the consecutive events, as in the following formula: $p(\text{final event}) = p1 \times p2 \times p \times \ldots \times pk$, where p1 is the probability of the first event in the scenario, p2 is the probability of the second, and so on. Therefore, even if the probabilities of components are high, the p(final event) can be low. For example, $.90 \times .80 \times .85 \times .80 \times .85 \times .90 = .37$.

A similar effect is true about estimating a probability of disjunction of events. This applies to situations when a decision maker is assessing the probability that at least one event out of a number of events will occur. We tend to underestimate the probability of disjunction of events. The probability that none will occur is $(1-p1) \times (1-p2) \ldots \times (1-pi)$. If the probabilities of six events are .10, .10, .15, .20, .15, and .10, $.90 \times .80 \times .85 \times .80 \times .85 \times .90 = .37$. Therefore, the probability that at least one of these events will occur is $1-.37 = .63$.

Method #5: Making Trade-offs

When trade-offs must be made (between cost and quality, for example), there is no objective optimal solution; instead, there is only consistency with one's goals and values. This is one of the reasons that this method is not widely used, as decision makers suggested to me during interviews. Another problem is that this technique works in situations when the consequences of each alternative are known before the decision is made, which is rarely the case[10].

This method has several strategies, which researchers in decision-making call "compensatory[5]." A compensatory strategy trades low values on one dimension against high values on another:

a. You can assign values to all constraints and then trade them against each other in *even swaps*. Assigning a value to constraints in order to produce even swaps is a creative and highly subjective process. You will be challenged if one constraint is about delivering a product on time, for example, and another is about the quality of the facility to be selected. When you are "stuck," however, you can benefit from this technique by going through the process and forcing yourself to contemplate the relative values that can be assigned to constraints.

b. Another strategy is the *ideal point model* in which each alternative is evaluated in terms of how far it is from the ideal point on each dimension. You can compile one evaluation indicator for each alternative by adding these numbers. This strategy encourages you to select the alternative with the lowest distance from the ideal point.

Analytical methods are extremely useful in evaluating your decision alternatives from different angles. Their value is not only in pointing you to a choice and offering a rationale for it, but also in providing you with information about your *reaction* to that choice. If rationally a choice looks good but your reaction to it is negative, you might need to dig deeper and understand the reasons for it. The following techniques in the Clarity State will help you do that.

> **Exercise**
>
> Which methods do you commonly use to educate your intuition on decision alternatives? If your arsenal consists of only one method, consider practicing another two evaluation methods.

After you have educated your intuition by analytical methods, the final call is your choice based on your gut feeling of what is right for you and the business.

Arriving at a Clear Choice

The gem cannot be polished without friction, nor man perfected without trials.
Chinese proverb

Reframing techniques, such as constraints relaxation, "shake up" the decision definition and may unearth other perspectives from which to look at options and, in fact, create additional solution alternatives.

Technique 1 in the following section serves as an intuitive assessment of potential solutions in terms of the fit between the problem statement after it has been "shaken up" and various alternatives. If reframing techniques are followed closely in time by solution sensitivity analysis, both sides of the decision map become clarified. When it is then followed by Technique 2 (solution alignment), the decision usually becomes clear. Therefore, I recommend using the techniques in this order.

I also have to stress that these techniques were applied after a decision maker went through the parts of the Clarity State Decision-Making process that we discussed in the previous chapters: building a decision map, balancing emotions, and clarifying a perspective on the decision. The combination of these techniques and their proper sequencing produces a breakthrough in arriving at a right choice.

In this exercise, it is important to pay attention to your emotions. Your emotions are your guides to a solution that is aligned with you. If you feel resistance relative to a solution alternative, acknowledge the feeling of resistance. Work with it until you understand its underlying reason in the way we discussed in Chapter 8, "Balancing Mind and Body—How to Learn from Your Emotional Cues." If you believe that you've found the right solution but it has significant risk, you might feel fear in proceeding with this solution. You will have to find a way to convert this fear into excitement and courage, because they are the opposite side of fear. The technique provides a way to accomplish this task by defining strategies for overcoming barriers to success.

Technique #1: Solution Sensitivity Analysis

In everything one must consider the end.
Jean de La Fontaine[11]

This technique consists of the following steps and has to be *applied to each solution option in turn*:

1. Reach and maintain the Clarity State.
2. Identify a key uncertainty associated with this solution.
3. Create the *most likely scenario* of how things will evolve after you execute this solution.

Use your imagination. Create a movie in your mind of how everything will evolve from the minute when you make this decision and select this option as a solution. How will you communicate it? Who is involved? What happens next? How do things evolve from there? Pay attention to the first associations that leap into your mind. What milestones do you see? They are important turning points in the implementation. How does the key uncertainty get resolved?

Stay away from assigning a specific probability to this scenario; focus instead on the future projection that is most natural for you.

4. Assess the worst-case scenario.

   Ask yourself: "What is the worst that can happen if the decision leads to negative business consequences?" Assess your reaction and acceptance level. Could you live through the worst if it were to happen? Prepare to accept this situation if it were to happen.

5. Identify reasons for failure.

   Notice how the key uncertainty turned out in the worst-case scenario. List other reasons for failure. What failure points led to the worst-case scenario? Do not dwell on this state of affairs too long. Just identify the problems.

   We learn much more from failure than from success. We often discover what we will do by finding out what we will not do. You make important discoveries when you make mistakes. It is much better to allow yourself to make these mistakes and learn from them in the playhouse of your mind rather than in real life.

   Having prepared yourself to accept the worst, ask yourself: "How can I improve on this solution so that the worst is avoided?" What can you do to avoid risks that you identified as reasons for failure?

   Again, create a movie in which creative solutions are implemented to address the risks at each turning point. Let your imagination fly.

6. Assess the best scenario.

   Now ask: "What is the best that can happen if I select this option?" Create another movie, this time of the best scenario. Pay attention to what is in the movie, what milestones you are seeing. Go over these mental pictures, delineate details, and make refinements. Play them over and over to yourself until you are satisfied.

PART V

7. Assess the fit with the objective and major constraints.

    I am not talking about rating the objective and all constraints rationally and then finding an option that has the best score. I am talking about the internal, intuitive signal about the fit of this solution to the problem that you are trying to resolve. How does it fit?

    You might get a reaction that surprises you, like "It doesn't fit very well to what I defined as a problem, but I like this solution—in fact, I know that this is the right choice!" Or "It seems like a good choice, but I really don't like it at all!" Pay attention, do not overrule these signals, do not rationalize them, make sure that you notice them, and then consider them.

8. Find solution adjustments.

    Contemplate: "Is there a way to tweak this solution to make it address the objective and the most important constraints better?" Because you have gone through the constraints relaxation exercise, you know the most important constraints, and you also know the problems that you have in addressing them in each option.

    Consider the following ways to develop adjustments:

    - Focus on what is good in this solution. Can you expand on this "goodness" to address the whole decision definition?

    - Or, on the contrary, find the detail in this option that is "clashing" with an important constraint. Look at other options; is there one option without this detail? Can you combine this solution with that option in a way that addresses the problematic constraint?

    - Consider stretching the solution over time (such as getting the payback over a period of time) or changing the strength or the scope of the solution to accommodate more constraints.

Consider Stanley's example.

EXAMPLE 12-2: STANLEY—EVALUATING MERGER PROPOSALS

Stanley runs a $200M public software company (RC). In the last six months, two competitors have approached the company with acquisition proposals. This process is coming to a head, with two offers on the table; both are similar in value and are considered to be "very good" by industry standards.

One offer is from Mercury—an all-stock offer from a smaller, less profitable competitor, a public company as well, but whose capitalization at this point is 1.7 times larger than RC's. Mercury's stock increased in price over the last six months. Stanley believes that this increase is due to the fact that Mercury has not done well in the last three years, but just recently the company became profitable and has remained profitable for the last few quarters.

The second offer is from Pluto, an $800M company, privately owned by a group of financial people who deal with distressed real estate with no knowledge of the industry. They have acquired five companies in the last 18 months.

Staying the course is also a very viable option. RC has also completed two acquisitions and has the stock power and the cash to acquire more companies. RC is a solid, profitable company with a good standing in the industry. Stanley is at the decision point. What to do—stay the course or take one of these offers?

One of the difficulties, of course, is comparing a cash offer to a stock offer from a shareholder's point of view, complicated by the fact that the offers come from companies of different caliber and characteristics. A stock offer might have a higher overall value, depending on how the market develops in the future. The cash offer provides immediate and rather good return to the shareholders.

The second difficulty is a disagreement on the board. The board consists of wealthy individuals who have had a long tenure on this board. Many have gifted their stock in the company to their children and grandchildren. At the moment, the board wants to stay the course, having seen the strength of the management team and the successes with prior acquisitions.

In Stanley's mind, however, the main consideration is shifts in the industry—the market is consolidating. He believes that players face a rocky road over the next two years. In addition, Microsoft has announced its intention to enter this specific market, which will slow customers' decision to buy from other vendors.

Stanley's decision map with key uncertainties for every option is shown in Figure 12-1.

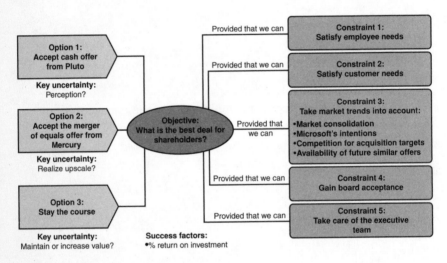

FIGURE 12-1

Stanley's Decision Map

As Stanley contemplates the constraints during the constraints relaxation exercise, he realizes that Constraints 1 and 2 will be equally addressed in all three options and should be taken out of consideration.

Even though the cash offer (Option 1) is good and provides shareholders with cash in their hands now, Stanley is unsure about the shareholders' reaction. Will they be happy? Or will they blame management for not accepting a deal with upscale potential? However, the shareholders' value per share in this case is certain and satisfies the success factor for the whole decision.

The key uncertainty of Option 2 (accepting a stock merger with a smaller company) is, in fact, the ability of shareholders to realize the upscale potential of the combined stock. Stanley is concerned that Mercury's stock may be overpriced at the moment. In addition, the combined company will be affected by the same market trends that make the future of the overall market unclear. Can shareholders cash out later at a significantly higher level? A downfall potential exists in this option—for not even achieving the success factor level of return that he set for this decision.

The board members are betting on the knowledge and experience of the current management team, including Stanley. They have steered the company well in the past. However, Stanley is concerned about the market trends he sees, especially the intensified competition from much larger rivals. Option 3, staying the course, assumes other acquisitions. However, fewer targets are available even now, not to mention that with consolidation, the price and competition for these targets will increase. The major uncertainty behind Option 3 is whether the company will be able to maintain and increase the shareholders' value on its own.

The probability tree that Stanley developed prior to the exercise clearly pointed in the direction of taking the offer from Mercury, because the stock offer was significantly higher than the cash offer. However, by slightly changing probabilities on the Mercury branch of the tree, the cash and stock offers could be made to almost tie in delivering value to shareholders. The stock offer, however, is obviously not certain, and cashing out will not be immediate for shareholders.

Contemplating the situation in the Clarity State and creating scenes associated with potential scenarios, Stanley realizes that his internal reaction to taking the stock offer is negative. His reaction to the outcomes of Option 3 (staying the course) is even worse.

Going through Technique 2 makes the decision clear and certain for him—he selects the cash offer (Option 1) to recommend to the board.

Stanley's case could have been simpler if it were not for the disagreement on the board. The disagreement was caused by the differences in how board members and Stanley made future projections about the attainment of the success factor (return on investment) in each option based on other parameters involved in the decision. For example, Stanley paid critical attention to market trends, judging them as having a negative impact on the company's ability to maintain or increase stock value in the staying-the-course scenario, versus one board member who discarded these trends altogether in his future projections. Based on his view, Stanley assigned lower probabilities to the solution of staying the course than did the director.

At the end of the day, if you are facing a choice involving uncertainty, you will have to take a risk, and what you risk will reveal what you value.

Technique #2: Finding the Best Solution Alignment

The wisest men follow their own direction.
Euripides[12]

Early on in the project, one CEO commented: "When the available options set off an internal signal which cries 'wrong,' I accept the need to give the decision more time. I start asking logical questions and testing my feeling of comfort/discomfort with the answers given." He then proceeded to explain that at the point when he has developed new options, he tries to find an option with the highest feeling of alignment with the problem and with him personally.

This description resonated with me because I have been using an options alignment technique for a number of years. The technique itself is very simple. However, it should be used after a thorough analysis of the decision problem and business implications of solution options, to prevent you from "shooting from the hip."

In this exercise, it is even more important to pay attention to your emotions. Look for a feeling of excitement or determination—an uplifting emotion that will enable you to fully embrace the solution and take it to a successful completion.

1. Reach and maintain the Clarity State.
2. Introduce all solution options into your awareness at the same time. You might want to assign symbols or specific scenes to each option and line them up in front of you. Keep the left side of the decision map in your mind's eye if this is easier for you.

3. Go from one solution to the next and assess your reaction. Do not think. Usually one of the outcomes will stand out from the others in some way. Watch for a feeling of excitement mounting. If it's there, in all likelihood, this is the option to choose.

4. If one option stands out, ask yourself: "Is this my decision?" Formulate your decision to yourself. Are you comfortable with it?

5. State to yourself: "I am ready to make a decision that is congruent with me and all the other parties involved."

This simple exercise can produce stunning results. Here are several comments from decision makers after the exercise:

"When you asked me to put the decision options in a line, I just kept the left-hand side of the decision map in my mind's eye. And as I was going from one outcome to the next, as I was instructed, one of the options stood out. I saw it lift up from the paper! The rest of the outcomes almost disappeared from the paper. They were in the background, as if written in lighter ink. I was surprised! I had a feeling that this alternative is definitely what I should take."

"I was not sure what to expect, but I followed your instructions to the letter. When you asked me to assign symbols to options, scenes came up in my mind with me as a main actor in these scenes that I was able to associate with each solution. As I was going from one solution to the next and back, one option became very vivid, and the scene became alive. It felt like I was there at that very moment! I could no longer see the other scenes. I was also surprised to find that I had a physical sensation of exhilaration in the area of my heart. I was certain that I am going to go do this! And this was unexpected—I did not anticipate having a reaction in my body!"

"Well, the scene that I associated with one option that I ended up selecting became like a movie. I was seeing myself as the solution implementation was evolving. I saw some very tiny details of what I should do at a particular step of the implementation project. The whole thing did not require any effort on my part; it was just there! Really, I believe that you cannot see the evolution of a path that is not your path; it is dim, and its evolution requires effort. You have to find the solution that you can visualize clearly, without effort."

Let's look at another example and take it through the process.

PART V

EXAMPLE 12-3: BOB—EXPANSION INTO SOUTH AMERICA

Bob is the CEO of a large manufacturing company that has decided to expand into South America. Market research data shows that there is an opportunity to enter South America ahead of the competition and capture a significant market share if the expansion is done properly. Bob is faced with this decision. His decision map with key uncertainties for every option appears in Figure 12-2.

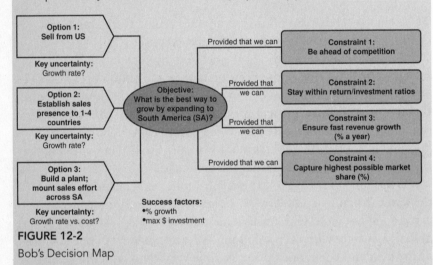

FIGURE 12-2

Bob's Decision Map

Bob has a number of concerns:

1. He wants to invest a certain amount of money and make it the most effective investment that will give the company the largest growth potential and highest market share.

2. He also believes that there is no time to waste. Even though competition for the company's products in South America is low at the moment, he knows that this will not be the case for long. Therefore, his company needs to move quickly.

His team has developed a spectrum of options starting from low investment—selling from the U.S.—to high investment of building a manufacturing plant in Argentina and mounting a full-scale sales effort in all major countries of South America. Bob is considering their recommendation to go with Option 2 and establish a local sales presence in three countries.

What happened?

As Bob goes through the solution sensitivity analysis exercise, considering outcomes based on the key uncertainties, he realizes that no option fits his decision definition well.

He agrees with the team that establishing sales presence in one to four countries (Option 2) will deliver on the parameters he posed to the team—growth acceleration and staying within cost boundaries. However, as he created scenes for a best scenario for this option, he saw himself talking to a happy customer in Brazil. In his words: "As the scene was playing out in my mind's eye, this customer told me that he was delighted with our great people working with him and with the quality of the products. He stressed, however, that he would be measuring us on the speed and flexibility of product delivery since it is critically important to his operation. It struck me at that point that we would not be able to deliver to his expectations, even though we took delivery flexibility into account in this option."

Bob was able to put himself into the shoes of a customer in Brazil and immediately realized that the developed product stocking options were insufficient to satisfy this customer's requirements. It's often the case that knowing the right way to get something done is virtually to have done it.

Bob was able to adjust this solution to fit his decision aim. He realized that he liked the major principle behind this option—namely, the company was reaching customers and closing deals across South America at the right rate. But the problem was that this option did not address customer delivery requirements. I asked him to look at other options and see if any of them addressed this issue. Obviously, having a full-scale manufacturing facility (Option 3) addresses this issue, but at a high investment that Bob was reluctant to currently commit to. This contemplation leads him to formulate a new option: the company should build a product assembly facility rather than the full-scale manufacturing operation but stay at the level defined in Option 2 in terms of the sales effort.

In his words: "The solution was so simple! I was not sure why I had not seen it before! Maybe it is because we had never done it before in this company. Historically, we always built full-scale plants..."

Going through Technique 2 (finding the best solution alignment), Bob becomes convinced that the option he just developed is the right option to pursue.

PART V

Exercise

Pull out your decision map. You are at the point of finalizing the decision you selected in Chapter 1, "The Key to Mastering Decisions." You might have made it already as you went through the Clarity State Decision-Making process in earlier chapters. This part establishes the internal alignment and confirms with certainty the rightness of the choice.

Reach the Clarity State and go through the solution sensitivity exercise followed by the outcome alignment. Record the steps of the techniques just discussed and play them back with adequate time between the steps.

Pay attention to your emotional reactions to different options. Notice which options you feel resistance to. Also notice which options you feel excited about. Record your impressions. Write down your final choice. You might want to revisit the discussion about characteristics of a clear decision in Chapter 1. Assess your reaction with respect to your final choice.

Make sure to turn off your rational thinking during the exercise. If you catch yourself saying "It is probably better for all concerned if we go with this option, because...", *stop*. You are not using the Clarity State to your advantage. Take a break, go for a walk, and then try again.

If you have not arrived at a clear choice, most likely you have not properly finished the steps we discussed in prior chapters. If you still feel strong emotions associated with the decision, go back to the techniques of working with the emotions. If you do not see a clear alternative, search for new perspectives. Most likely, you are still framed. Work on creating more solution options. Read Appendix B on reducing decision complexity—it might help you identify decision layers and the right level of detail at each layer. Then, come back and do this exercise again.

Process for Clarifying Your Choice

Courage is resistance to fear, mastery of fear—not absence of fear.
Mark Twain[13]

In summary, arriving at a clear choice requires vision power and courage to proceed with the alternative that you consider right for the business. This part of the Clarity State Decision-Making process serves as a culmination of all prior decision contemplation from different angles. Having gone through defining the decision, searching for new perspectives, and then evaluating solutions, finding the best solution alignment becomes easy. This part of the process finalizes the selection and establishes clarity.

This process summarizes the techniques presented in this chapter:

- Educate your intuition with data and analysis. Use one or more analytical methods to evaluate solution options.
- Be in the Clarity State.
  - Perform solution sensitivity analysis. For each solution alternative:
    - Identify key uncertainties.
    - Consider the most likely scenario.
    - Accept the worst.
    - Identify reasons for failure, and prepare to avoid them.
    - Develop the best scenario.
    - Assess the fit between this solution and the decision aim.
  - Find your preferred solution by listening to your emotions.
  - Finalize your choice. Commit to the implementation.

Key Point

In order to reach clarity faster and easier, develop your vision power. Use Clarity State as your spring platform, and use imagination and visualization as tools and emotions as your guide. Vision power is a skill that is developed with practice.

Executives are paid for making decisions. Many of these decisions are not pleasant or popular. If it were otherwise, they would have been made already. Effective decisions require courage to take a stance that others are unwilling to take. Making a clear decision with total internal alignment establishes commitment and enables you to lead with passion and vision.

CHAPTER 13

Voilà!—How to Put It All Together

And herein lies the secret of true power. Learn, by constant practice, how to husband your resources, and concentrate them, at any moment, upon a given point.
James Allen[1]

This book rests on three premises:

- Similar to an athlete whose mastery is evident when he or she competes to break a record, the mastery of an accomplished decision maker is evident when he or she has to make a tough decision.

- The key to achieving decision-making mastery is the ability to effectively focus your physical, mental, and emotional resources at will on a certain issue.

- Such focus enables you to reach decision clarity faster, more easily, and with greater certainty. It is a skill and can be learned.

The objective of this book has been to identify and describe ways and techniques that stimulate you to learn for yourself how to become a master decision maker and how to reach clarity on difficult strategic decisions.

My approach combines traditional, rational ways that we usually use in making decisions with innovative mind-focusing techniques that enable you to access more brainpower than you normally do. The intent is to replicate an effect experienced by a person in a clarity moment—when things fall into place and a path of action becomes clear in an instant.

This book presents a practical technique—Clarity State Decision-Making—that can be used by decision makers in small and large organizations alike to make difficult decisions.

Appendix A, "Clarity State Decision-Making Techinque—A Summary," summarizes all the major processes of this technique. I am providing it in response to many requests from decision makers I've worked with. They wanted to have a brief summary of the technique to carry around with them after reading the book. You can use it whenever you are working on a particular decision or strategy and you find yourself at the airport or some other place where you have downtime. With the summary, you can use your time productively, structuring your decision and contemplating it.

The following example traces the Clarity State Decision-Making technique from beginning to end—from when I arrived in Mitch's office to discuss his decision to the minute he made it, less than an hour later.

EXAMPLE 13-1: MITCH—NEW PRODUCT INTRODUCTION

Mitch is the CEO of a midsize healthcare services company that has undergone a number of revamps under his leadership. Mitch is concerned that the current strategy won't achieve the targeted growth results. On the other hand, his company just completed the development of a new and exceptionally innovative product. The product is in a "disruptive" category—it's unique in the marketplace. Even though market indications are good, the product may do exceptionally well or fail miserably. But it is certain to cannibalize his company's other product lines. Mitch has to decide when, how, and at what price to introduce this product to the market.

When I arrived at his office, Mitch told me about his decision and how he was trying to decide which way to proceed. He would get to his office, sit down, and pull out the folder in which he had been collecting materials related to the decision and go through it again. He and his team did the homework. This folder contained financial projections, pros and cons lists, and a probability tree. He had also received advice from his board members and trusted advisors. However, reviewing the material again did not make the decision any clearer.

He said that he would usually end up thinking about people with whom he could discuss this issue. The problem was that he had been over the situation with most of his advisors several times and knew what they would tell him. There was practically nobody else he could turn to.

Usually, he would sit there for a little longer and then shut the folder with mounting frustration and decide to put "this mess" aside for just a couple hours longer. "It will come to me, I'm sure," he would think, and then he would get up and throw himself into operational issues that had been waiting for him.

I explained the Clarity State Decision-Making process to Mitch and showed him the software to measure the attainment of the Clarity State. The software was used in meetings such as this one to ensure that the decision maker has reached a certain level of physical, mental, and emotional coherence before decision contemplation. Mitch had no problem reaching the Clarity State quickly, because he normally practices relaxation techniques, so he found the process similar to what he regularly uses. We then started working on Part II of the technique—decision definition. I asked Mitch to state how he defines his decision and name an objective and constraints. The following is Mitch's initial decision definition.

EXAMPLE 13-1 CONTINUED: PART II—INITIAL DECISION DEFINITION

Main objective: Successful product introduction

Constraint 1: Achieve higher growth

Constraint 2: Minimize risk of other products' cannibalization

In our discussion, Mitch shared his concerns. This decision had profound implications for the company's future. It felt to Mitch like a "betting the company" type of decision. Mitch believed that their cash position was not strong. If he selected a strategy that was unsuccessful, they would need to raise additional money. His major worry, however, was the aftermath of the product introduction. He was certain that the competition would introduce products of the same kind, and rather quickly. His other product lines would be weakened. "Maybe we should just forget about this product and focus on our main product lines," he said, sharing his doubts with me.

After listening to Mitch's concerns, it was not surprising to me that Mitch considered this decision difficult. We discussed the fact that these concerns have to be reflected in the decision definition—the idea that Mitch embraced. He also agreed that, more importantly, if he did not address these concerns in the eventual solution, they could serve as barriers to a successful implementation.

We worked through the steps of Part II—defining a decision. He made major changes to his initial definition. He realized that higher growth (his initial Constraint 1) *is* the main objective behind this introduction.

He also added two concerns as constraints to the decision map in addition to the initial subobjective that was represented by Constraint 2—minimize risk of other products' cannibalization. In summary, he had two major concerns—the company's weak cash position, and the fear that competition could quickly introduce a similar product, even though Mitch's company had patented the product. In accordance with the process of clarifying constraints, he reworded concerns into positive, constructive subobjectives, changing "a weak cash position" into "satisfy financial parameters" and "a fear of a similar competitive product introduction" into "Be first to market and maintain product differentiation."

After adding four solution options, Mitch finalized his decision map, as shown in Figure 13-1.

Decision: Product Introduction Strategy

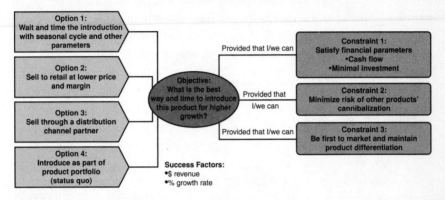

FIGURE 13-1

Mitch's First Decision Map

Mitch was definitely emotional about his decision. And understandably so, because he felt that he was making a "bet the company" type of decision. We started working on Part III of the process—dealing with emotions. The following is Mitch's feedback after this exercise in the Clarity State.

EXAMPLE 13-1 CONTINUED: PART III—DEALING WITH EMOTIONS

"As you asked me to find the emotions associated with the decision, I realized how scared I was that I would make the wrong call. I was totally in the grip of this fear. This fear was manifesting throughout my body—unpleasant sensations in my stomach, around my heart, and a terrible strain in the neck! It took me awhile to find the visualization that eased the pain. Then, I suddenly realized that the fear has to do with the uncertainty about product performance in the market. As you suggested, I worked on finding a way to address this fear somehow and formulate it as a constraint, in positive, constructive terms. It worked! I felt immediately better about this decision!"

Mitch added a fourth constraint to his decision definition to address his fear about the product performance: "See results within three months." He reasoned that if the product did not show signs of being successful, they could stop the investment and pull it back from the market. His updated decision map is shown in Figure 13-2.

Decision: Product Introduction Strategy

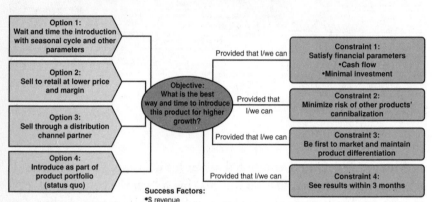

FIGURE 13-2
Mitch's Updated Decision Map

Mitch shared with me that he was feeling much better about the decision and was confident that the company should proceed with an introduction. At what time, how, and at what price were still unclear.

We proceeded with Part IV of the technique—achieving clarity of perspective. The following is Mitch's feedback about this part of this process.

EXAMPLE 13-1 CONTINUED:
PART IV—CONSTRAINTS RELAXATION

"As you asked me whether the first constraint is real or perceived, I suddenly realized that the root cause of my fear is the fact that we do not have the financial strength to fund the introduction. It is an obvious fact, but somehow I wanted to bootstrap and self-fund it. I totally ruled raising money out of my mind. In fact, when my CFO suggested this path of action, I yelled at him. But, in reality, the part of Constraint 1 (minimize investment) is a perceived constraint—we can and should raise money for this product introduction! If we do not promote the product well, we can jeopardize the effort.

"When you asked me to maximize Constraint 2, which has to do with minimizing the risk to other product lines as a result of this introduction, I suddenly realized that we can be creative here. We offer these products only through our internal distribution. We can offer them through several distributors. This action will bring us additional revenue. Why didn't we think of this before?

"Then you asked me to maximize Constraint 3, which has to do with dealing with competition. I was really worried that our main competitor can introduce a 'variation on our theme' and confuse the market. If this happens, they would be leveraging our marketing investment. As I was thinking about this and how to prevent it, I realized that we can utilize the other innovations that we are working on into a series of introductions—there is no way that our competitors will be able to do this as well!"

During this simple exercise, Mitch shifted his perspective on the decision three times. He had three insights that changed how he was thinking about the decision. Clearing out a perceived constraint will enable Mitch to have more financial flexibility. He found a way to get additional revenue from existing products—an action that was prevented by a frame that had been based on the company's history. And finally, he found a way to deal with competition by leveraging other innovations within the company that he and his team never considered in the context of this product.

The request to identify the crux of the issue introduced another perspective.

EXAMPLE 13-1 CONTINUED:
PART IV—IDENTIFYING THE CRUX OF THE ISSUE

"I realized that the crux of this decision is the pricing level that we are willing to accept for this product. If we apply the current pricing structure to this product, it would be priced out of the retail channel. The company, however, has no experience with lower product prices and with working through retail."

Working with another technique of Part IV, expanding his view of the decision, Mitch found yet another perspective.

EXAMPLE 13-1 CONTINUED: PART IV—EXPANDING HIS VIEW

"This part was useful to me because I remembered why I am in this business to begin with. I selected this business due to its positive impact on people's lives.

"I imagined the business three years from now. A very positive picture just shaped in my mind—how this product catapulted us into the leading position in the market. I became totally charged with our purpose and felt that we are doing the right thing by introducing this product. Suddenly, the price did not seem to matter."

At this point of the process, Mitch shared with me that he was becoming clearer on the overall situation and was almost certain what he had to do. We proceeded with the Part V technique of evaluating solution alternatives.

EXAMPLE 13-1 CONTINUED:
PART V—EVALUATING SOLUTION OPTIONS

"I ruled out Option 1 (wait for the right seasonal cycle) immediately. The value of timing it seasonally is marginal. As I was considering reasons for failure in Option 2 (selling through the retail channel), I decided that we should get additional retail expertise, since we are limited from that point of view.

"Working with a distribution partner (Option 3) was appealing to me because a solid partner would bring additional expertise in marketing as well as the existing customer base. However, the way we put together the option was too limiting. We were considering only one particular distribution partner with almost an exclusive deal. In order to make this option viable and to satisfy our revenue and margin parameters, we need to completely rework the approach, take out exclusivity, and identify and sign up more partners. I realized that we had more to lose than to gain by going this route without proper preparation.

"I think that something changed as I worked through the prior parts of the process, because 'going with the status quo' (Option 4) was no longer an option for me. Maybe it is because I dealt with my fear constructively."

In summary, at the end of this evaluation process, Mitch left "retail option" (Option 2) and "distribution option" (Option 3) as viable options. Option 3 required more refinement to make it workable. The deal with the distribution partner would need to be revised, and other partners would need to be identified and signed up. Option 2 was viable, but the price level was still not clear to Mitch.

Mitch and I looked at the financial projections that were created by his team assuming different levels of product pricing. I observed that Mitch paid closer attention to the scenarios with higher product pricing—the ones that assumed the product pricing was over $150. One part remained in the Clarity State Decision-Making process—finding the best solution alignment—and we decided to proceed with it.

EXAMPLE 13-1 CONTINUED: THE MOMENT OF INSIGHT
PART V—FINDING THE BEST SOLUTION ALIGNMENT

"When you asked me to put the decision options in a row, I just kept the left-hand side of the decision map in my mind's eye. And as I was going from one outcome to the next, as I was instructed,

> Option 2 (selling through retail) stood out! The rest of the outcomes almost disappeared from the paper. They were in the background, as if done in lighter ink. I was surprised!
>
> "A number, $49.95, flashed in front of me. The number stunned me! I would have never picked this number by myself! It's too low—even $89.95 is low for me. But I felt that this was the right number to go with and that the second option was the right strategy! I had a feeling that the highlighted option is definitely what we should do."

Mitch had fears, concerns, and awareness of risks associated with a solution option. He probably knew subconsciously that the price level that was required by the market for this product to be successful would have to be low. Through this process, he was able to face his fears and put them aside. This time he got charged with positive momentum behind the strategy, accepting all its risks and being ready to deal with them.

Mitch reached clarity on his decision within an hour. He had been "wrestling" with this decision for the last three months. Two things made it possible: one, being in the Clarity State, and two, contemplating his decision in a way that combines rational and intuitive approaches. This approach combines decision-making best practices, analytical evaluations, imagination, visualization, and intuitive reactions.

This example demonstrates how the process works overall from definition to resolution. Each decision maker experiences it differently.

Key Point
Decision-making mastery can be reached by using the Clarity State as the platform and Clarity State Decision-Making as the process.

In looking back on the observations and the flow of the chapters, another quite different aspect of decision-making emerges.

Key Point
Decision-making is about self-discipline. You cannot achieve decision-making mastery without self-observation and self-development.

Many of us never question our decision-making style until we are faced with a particularly tough decision with dire consequences. When we stop to look, we rarely find a method. Instead, we usually find a big mess. We discover that sometimes we make random choices or that decisions are made for us by outside circumstances, and we just comply. Sometimes we make decisions by abdicating our power to a set of rules built into some analytical method or by rebelling against what is expected of us. And sometimes we decide because we feel like it or create an unrealistic picture in our mind that we fall in love with. Reaching mastery in decision-making requires being aware of our current methods and having the interest and drive to improve them. In other words, it requires self-discovery and self-discipline. The following elements are important:

1. **Know where you stand.** The first step toward decision-making mastery is procedural: recording your decisions and how you make them. Similar to recording your time, recording your decision will give you critical information about how you learned to make decisions in your early years. By itself, however, it will not bring any advance toward decision-making mastery.

2. **Be introspective.** By analyzing your decision-making record, you will be able to identify your most common difficulties in making decisions. It will raise searching questions about your stance on certain issues, your personal goals versus organizational goals. This requires a high degree of introspection and the willingness and comfort level to be introspective. What are you doing well? Is there a pattern to issues that you encounter? What barriers are you creating on your way to your own success? In my experience, all great leaders are introspective.

3. **Leverage the Clarity State.** You can make many improvements to your decision-making style without using the Clarity State. However, you will find that Clarity State can make it easier to identify and make these improvements.

    Clarity State by itself is a very enjoyable and powerful state. Its definition is based on methods used by athletes in achieving peak performance and research in the fields of neuroscience and psychology. The tremendously positive impact of this state on the ease and speed of the decision-making process has been verified in working meetings with decision makers who were actively engaged in making current decisions.

    Clarity State can also be used to reflect on your overall decision-making style and defining adjustments. Because you developed your style over a lifetime, it is a habit by now, and issues with it might not be visible to you without the Clarity State. Reflect on the patterns of your past decisions. Do you see a particular thing that you worry about in every decision, for example? Was worrying about it worth it? Could you have changed your process to address this concern in a different way?

    Spending time finding your own Clarity State and learning to get into it before making decisions will pay you back enormously in speed and quality of decisions. It can also pay tremendously in the overall decision-making process improvement if you leverage this state for reflecting on your style. More importantly, I believe that it will also pay back in increased peace of mind, compared to the anxiety and tension that we come to accept as our normal state of being these days.

4. **Develop mind discipline and focus.** Based on my meetings with decision makers, I concluded that, in order to utilize Clarity State to your advantage in decision-making, you need to learn how to use your mind differently and master a higher-than-normal level of mind focus and discipline.

    Mind focus and control are required to maintain a coherent state of mind, body, and emotions *while* considering a decision. This decision consideration (or contemplation, as I call it) is a significantly different process from our regular rational thinking.

Decision contemplation in the Clarity State is most effective when your system is in balance between the intuitive and the rational, allowing your rational thinking to step into the background and getting the intuitive to step forward, giving a reaction to all the rationales that are being considered. Mind discipline and control are required in maintaining mental flexibility, a high level of mental observation and openness in allowing new ideas and insights into your conscious awareness. They are also required in not responding to ideas in a habitual manner and instead rationalizing new and interesting thoughts. Most importantly, mind discipline is required in maintaining a sharp and complete mental focus on the issue at hand throughout the decision contemplation and disregarding unrelated thoughts when they come in.

CEOs who run larger companies, I observed, exhibit higher levels of mind discipline and control, which is not surprising because this ability is developed with experience. Personally, I correlate a person's level of mental control with the level of achievement that person reaches in his or her career.

Key Point
The effort of developing high-level mind discipline can pay you back in higher achievement in your career.

Learning to use Clarity State for decision-making (maintaining the state while contemplating a decision) will set the stage for new insights, ideas, and unexpected breakthroughs, as I observed during my work with decision makers.

5. **Adopt best practices.** The great thing about the subject of making decisions is that you can always do better. You can never get bored. You can focus on improving your decision-making style step-by-step by using techniques presented in this book.

The presented techniques are intended to trigger insight about the situation related to a decision in a similar way that a thought or a feeling triggers insights in a clarity moment. These techniques are based on research into the main reasons behind difficulties in making tough choices and best practices for overcoming them that were collected during interviews.

The following collected best practices for overcoming decision difficulties are shared throughout this book:

- A decision definition method and a graphical decision representation in a one-page decision map
- Techniques of dealing with emotions and balancing emotion with reason
- Techniques of finding alternative perspectives on a situation and redefining a decision frame
- Methods of finding an alignment with a solution

The improvement you decide to incorporate into your style may be small, but with it, your leap to decision-making mastery can be large. For example, you might learn to define your decisions better. The mere awareness of critical decision parameters will bring additional depth to the overall process. Or you might learn to expertly shift frames. This alone can clarify many decisions for you.

I believe that just adopting these methods into one's decision-making process will bring great advantages in speed and ease of decision-making, as you have seen through many examples in this book.

The most powerful recipe for improvement, however, is the combination of being in the Clarity State supported by the discipline of decision definition and methods of overcoming decision difficulties. This combination enables deep insights and breakthrough ideas to surface. With practice, you can unleash this innate power of insight on any issue, problem, or forward-looking strategy.

6. **Stretch yourself and have fun.** Without challenges, life is boring. Remember that if you were declared a decision-making master today, there would be no decision challenges to face. You likely would get bored. Take it as a game. Have fun with it. Observe yourself, and invent more powerful methods that work for you. If you are having fun at this game, you will be better at it, and you will experience less confusion and more clarity. It works.

Utilizing the Clarity State Decision-Making process, you will be able to reach clarity faster, more easily, and with greater certainty. Clear decisions enable clear communication. Furthermore, clarity in decisions enables you to lead with passion and conviction. Great leaders are known for this skill. Biographers of former President Ronald Reagan stress again and again that he was able to quickly reach clarity, arriving at a choice that he felt was right for him and the country.

Following this process for your decisions will enable you to eliminate confusion and dramatically increase clarity in your decision-making.

I know that there are enough adventurous decision makers in the world who will experiment with the Clarity State, learn to reach it, and use this wonderful and powerful state for decision-making.

Clarity State Decision-Making Technique— A Summary

Root causes behind decision difficulties are:

- Lack of a clear objective
- Lack of clear constraints
- Difficulty in dealing with emotions
- Lack of a clear perspective
- Difficulty in selecting from among options

Clarity State is the state of being

- Physically relaxed
- Emotionally positive, happy, released from fear and anxiety
- Charged with power, success, self-confidence, and energy
- Totally in the present
- Mentally focused on the task at hand

Clarity State Decision-Making Process

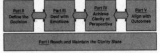

Part I: Reach and maintain the clarity state. Utilizing breathing and mind-focusing techniques, reach a coherent state of mind, body, and emotions quickly and at will, whenever you need to make a decision.

Part II: Define the decision. Create a one-page decision map that captures the most salient factors related to the decision at the right level of detail.

Part III: Deal with emotions. Identify, acknowledge, and utilize emotions related to the decision to clarify the issues involved.

Part IV: Achieve clarity of perspective. Utilize several techniques, such as constraints relaxation, to identify, evaluate, and select the right way to look at the decision.

Part V: Align with outcomes. Reflect on the solution options in turn in such a way that it becomes clear that one option is the right solution.

Part I: Technique of Reaching the Clarity State

Step 1: Prepare.

- Sit quietly in a comfortable position, preferably with your back straight.
- Close your eyes and look up about 20 degrees behind your eyelids. This helps you relax and focus easier.

Step 2: Relax your body.

- Start breathing deeply and slowly. It should feel like a sigh on the exhale. Imagine that the tension is coming out of you with each exhale.
- Scan your body. If you find tension anywhere, breathe through this tension and relax it.

Step 3: Calm your mind.

- Pick a word, sound, or phrase, such as "relax," and say it to yourself on the exhale.

Step 4: Clear your mind.

- When thoughts arrive, do not get involved with them; simply say to yourself, "I'll deal with it later," and return to your breathing and repetition.

Step 5: Charge up.

- Recall a situation when you felt totally happy. Re-experience it with as many senses as possible.

- Now recall an experience where you felt very successful, self-confident, excited, or on top of the world, with a "no barriers exist for me" feeling. Relive it as vividly as possible, with as many senses as possible involved. Get into this feeling of excitement, self-power, and success.

Part II: Define the Decision

Decision Definition = Objective + Constraints
Decision Map = Decision Definition + Solution Options

Decision Map

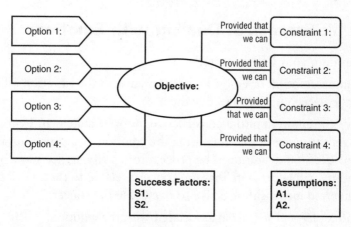

Process for Clarifying a Decision Objective

- Start with the decision question.

- Ask "Why is this important?" several times until you get to a fundamental reason behind this decision connected to the vision of the business.

- Focus on *one* parameter in your objective.
- Incorporate the decision question into the objective. Formulate the objective starting with "What is the best way to...".
- Identify success metrics.

Process for Clarifying Decision Constraints

- Compile a list of concerns.
  - List easily identifiable concerns by asking "Why is this decision difficult for me?"
  - Review commonly overlooked areas of concern for missing factors.
  - Identify emotional, motivational, and other concerns.
- Convert each concern into an objective to overcome the concern.
- Make sure to use an action verb in defining an objective, such as *satisfy*, *improve*, *address*, *generate*, or *enable*.
- Tie decision constraints to the decision objective with "provided that I/we can...".
- Identify and remove perceived or false constraints.

Part III: Process of Dealing with Emotions

- Maintain your Clarity State.
- Find an emotion or emotions associated with the situation related to the decision. Acknowledge them.
- Shift the emotion into a constructive, positive statement by formulating the concern that is causing the emotion as a constraint in your decision definition. The process for clarifying decision constraints will necessitate that the concern related to the emotion be converted into a subobjective to *overcome* the concern.
- Find a physical sensation associated with the emotion.
- Use the physical sensation as an instrument to find the emotional balance point. Work with visualization exercises, and select the one that lessens the physical sensation.

Part IV: Process of Achieving Clarity of Perspective

- Be in the Clarity State.
- Relax constraints.
- Stretch assumptions.
- Look for a crux of the issue.
- Stand back; find a broader viewpoint.
- Shift a loss into a gain.
- See the decision successfully implemented.

Part V: Process of Aligning with Outcomes

- Educate your intuition with data and analysis. Use one or more analytical methods to evaluate solution options.
- While in the Clarity State:
  - Perform solution sensitivity analysis. For each solution alternative:
    - Identify key uncertainties.
    - Consider the most likely scenario.
    - Accept the worst.
    - Identify reasons for failure, and prepare to avoid them.
    - Develop the best scenario.
    - Assess the fit between this solution and decision aim.
  - Find your preferred solution by listening to your emotions.
  - Finalize your choice. Commit to the implementation.

In order to reach decision clarity, develop your vision power. Use Clarity State as your spring platform, imagination and visualization as tools, and emotions as your guide.

If you have a complex decision, separate a communications layer and one or two other layers focused on the most critical aspects of the decision.

Additional Tips on Reducing Decision Complexity

Simplicity is an acquired taste. Mankind, left free, instinctively complicates life.
Katharine Fullerton Gerould[1]

Complex decisions are multilayered. Decision makers are usually unaware of this fact and attempt to solve all the layers at the same time, thus increasing the difficulty of the decision. By finding a way to "peel" off decision layers and focus on each layer separately, the decision complexity can be dramatically reduced. I call this decision de-layering.

By identifying a decision layer, you can zoom in on a particular aspect of the decision, consider it with its own constraints and solution options, and then zoom out to the higher level with useful observations about the inner layer. In essence, decision de-layering allows a "zoom in, zoom out" way of looking at a decision.

A communications layer is one obvious example of a decision layer. However, as a norm, we almost never separate the decision itself from communication of the decision. Finding other aspects of the decision that are worth focusing on in a separate layer is even trickier.

If you have defined your decision and completed the Clarity State decision-making process but are not yet at the clarity point, the following techniques will help you identify problematic aspects of your decision and de-layer and clarify them. Usually, when you come back to the top decision layer with the lessons learned from contemplating the deeper layers, your choice becomes obvious.

Clarity of Communication

When a thought is too weak to be expressed simply, it should be rejected.
Marquis de Vauvenargues[2]

Making a decision and communicating it to the people concerned are two different things, even though they are interrelated, sometimes very tightly. Unfortunately, this interrelationship, if not consciously addressed, can block your progress on arriving at a decision.

In working with decision makers, I saw a number of cases when communication issues involved in decisions complicated decisions themselves.

Key Point
It is one thing to find a solution that is aligned with a decision maker. It is a completely different thing to communicate this decision.

A lot of times, if you don't separate these two issues, the decision becomes much more complex.

EXAMPLE B-1: KATE—DELAYING MAKING A PERSONNEL DECISION

Kate, the president of a public company, has worked with Amy for the last ten years. Amy has helped her in a number of tough situations with loyalty, passion, and commitment. Kate took the presidency just a few months ago, and her previous position is open. Amy believes that she is a great candidate to fill this position, and even though Kate and Amy have not talked about it, Amy behaves as if the position is hers. Kate, on the other hand, is considering bringing in a candidate from the outside. She also believes that another person on the team is actually better qualified for this position than Amy.

Kate said that the decision itself was actually easy when she realized that she preferred an internal candidate due to the steep learning curve required for the job as well as the fact that the other candidate was the better choice. Her difficulty was that she "dreaded" the moment of explaining the decision to Amy. In thinking about the decision, she also thought about the probable outcome of Amy's leaving the team after she did not receive this promotion. Because Kate continued to "wrap these things into the decision itself," the decision lingered for months, even though it was a clear decision.

Sound familiar? Actually, I've heard similar stories from decision makers a number of times. In fact, this seems to be a common mistake—not separating the decision itself from the communication of the decision.

When I asked Kate how she resolved the issue, she said that it was the focus on the business objective—it was clear to her that the other candidate was better for the job.

Best Practice   **One of the ways to reduce decision complexity is to consciously separate the decision itself from the communication of the decision.**

In my work with decision makers, I developed a simple technique—separating the decision itself and the communication of the decision into different decision layers.

Let's demonstrate this technique on Kate's decision. Kate's decision map is shown in Figure B-1.

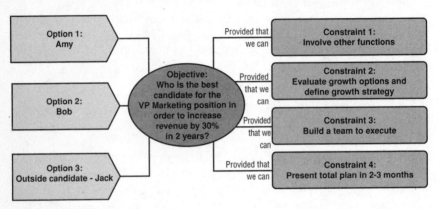

FIGURE B-1
Kate's Decision Map

As you can see, the constraints in the decision itself are related to various major concerns that Kate is trying to address by filling the position of VP of Marketing on her team.

Because Kate was in this position previously, she has intimate knowledge of the challenges that the new person will face:

- The market is shifting, and the old strategy needs to be rethought and changed; otherwise, the company's growth will stagnate. Her team has started working on a number of growth options, but they need deeper analysis and evaluation.

- Kate believes that one of the success factors lies in uncovering specific strengths from other functions and leveraging them in the market. For example, the company has been beating competitors on the cycle time of deliveries. Her question is—can we ride on this? Can we make it an even stronger differentiation? In order to explore this, the Marketing VP will have to develop and sustain a much tighter relationship with other functions in the business than what exists right now.

- Kate also knows that the marketing team as it exists right now will have to be upgraded for the new challenges, and she needs a person who can do it.

- Last, the challenge is that the new person will have to move really quickly—Kate would like to see the complete plan in a couple of months, not longer than three.

Kate has three options: Amy, her coworker for ten years; Bob, whom she brought onboard a year ago and has been evaluating by giving him challenging assignments; and Jack, a talented outside candidate.

As Kate considers the whole situation, it becomes clear that the speed with which she would like this effort to move forward precludes her from even looking at Jack's candidacy. He is from the same industry but will have to ramp up his knowledge of the product and the operations—not enough time to have a plan in three months. So, her choice is really between Amy and Bob. Amy is creative and very intelligent, but she will be challenged to build a good team and create tight relationships with other functions—both requirements fundamental for the job. Bob is clearly the better choice. "It's clear!" she says.

Kate's immediate reaction when turning to the issue of communicating this decision to Amy is: "I really don't want to think about it! I don't want her to leave!"

After much resistance, Kate forces herself to think about it. She decides that the objective is "What is the best way to communicate this decision to Amy in order to retain her?" She lists her concerns and starts putting them as constraints on a separate decision map. Kate's communications layer decision map is shown in Figure B-2.

She realizes that in fact there is a way to retain Amy—by showing her a role in the team that she will find exciting, that will address her growth needs and leverage her skills. As Kate contemplates this angle, several options appear. Kate wanted to consider acquiring a couple companies that were "a perfect fit with us," but she did not have anybody to lead the effort. Then, there are two other urgent efforts that Amy can lead and "do a great job." As Kate continues to think in the same vein, her excitement is mounting—she is now certain that she can find a way to retain Amy.

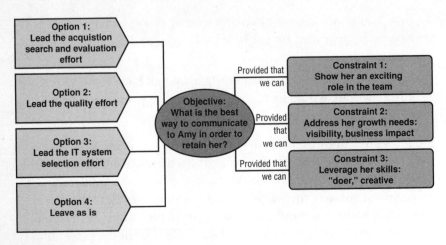

FIGURE B-2

Kate's Decision—Communication Layer Decision Map

By separating the communication aspect of the decision into a separate layer, Kate developed a creative way to address her concerns about talking to Amy about her choice.

Kate created a communications layer *after* she became clear on the overall decision. The following technique recommends this order. However, I found that sometimes it is useful to engage in developing the communications layer decision map *at the same time* as the overall decision map. Becoming clear on your communication is always a good practice, but it might not be the barrier for this particular decision. You want to focus your de-layering time on the aspects of the decision that are problematic. Completing the cycle of decision contemplation on the overall decision usually identifies problematic aspects that might require de-layering.

Technique: Creating a Communication Decision Layer

Building a communications layer requires a different focus—not on the decision itself but on all aspects related to the communication of your decision: ways to communicate the motivation and intent behind the decision, current perspectives of the people involved, their expectations, their potential reaction to the decision, how to best address this reaction, and clear articulation of implementation expectations and requirements.

1. Create a decision map of your decision; focus on the aspects of the decision that are business-related, disregarding the communication aspect and emotions associated with this aspect, if applicable.

2. Find the "right" solution for you at this level of detail by completing all parts of the Clarity State Decision-Making process. Focus on contemplating business objectives and all the relevant constraints. Stay away from thinking about communications.

3. Create a communications layer in which the focus is on concerns related to the best way to explain and get buy-in of your decision to all parties. Use Clarity State where appropriate. If you believe more than one party will disagree or have difficulties accepting your decision, you might want to create separate layers for each such party. Use the same decision map building process as you did for the decision itself. Take the following best practices into account:

   a. Consider the issue from each party's point of view. In fact, one of CEOs I worked with put himself in the shoes of the Senior VP on his staff and created a decision map from his perspective. This exercise was very instructive because the CEO realized specific concerns that the VP could have and how they could be addressed.

   b. Make sure that you clearly describe the business purpose and intent and your motivation behind the decision.

   c. There is also clarity of agreement. On every level of personal and interpersonal relationships, in every business relationship, in every venture and group, there are unspoken agreements. The more those unspoken agreements can be spoken, the clearer you will be. If you are working with someone, be clear on the agreements between you and this party. If they are not written down, make sure that they are clearly voiced. Many problems can happen when agreements are not clear, when one person follows one set of agreements and another follows another.

Key Point

Clarity of communication means being precise and accurate in describing your decision. When you are clear on your purpose, your intent, your motivation, and your agreements, you can reflect this clarity in your communication, and then action flows.

Exercise

Create a communications layer for the decision you chose in Chapter 1, "The Key to Mastering Decisions." Consider people involved and their expectations and reactions. Be clear on business intent and your motivation behind the decision. What is the best way to communicate your decision?

Reducing Decision Complexity by Creating Decision Layers

Divide each of the difficulties into as many parts as possible and as may be required in order to resolve them better.
René Descartes[3]

Separating a communications layer into a separate layer is only one instance of de-layering decisions and reducing their complexity.

You can create a decision layer for any aspect of the decision that has more depth than other issues. Each layer has its own decision definition that has to be carefully thought through. The focus on a smaller part of the decision enables you to surface and answer questions that may not be visible at a higher layer. When these questions are addressed, the overall decision becomes clear.

Let's demonstrate this process on Example 3-6 (Jack's decision), which was discussed in Chapter 3, "Five Hurdles to Clarity." The decision was about selecting a way to transition the company's products to a new technology platform. Jack's decision map appears in Figure B-3.

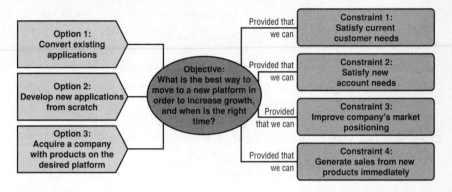

FIGURE B-3
Jack's Product Platform Decision Map

As you remember, Jack's difficulty is that all options appear viable. In fact, the company marched in the direction of all three options simultaneously. The team selected a conversion tool and installed it, and it was working. Thirteen of 52 applications were converted and were functional. A "development from scratch" team was put together to explore and estimate a timeline for developing applications from scratch. It developed projections on the length of time that would be required to rewrite all 52 applications. MP has also screened the market for a potential acquisition target from afar and had information that MP's product suite was much broader and deeper than anything else on the market.

Jack decided to abandon the conversion as well as the development-from-scratch effort and acquire a company with a proven set of applications on a new platform. The decision came as a surprise to Jack as well as to the board. Here is the process of how Jack arrived at the decision.

As Jack was wrestling with this decision, he kept thinking about his customer base. He isolated his question as "Would my current customers accept the application, and if so, when?" MP's customer base consists of mostly slow adopters of technology; in many cases, they are "owner-influenced management style" companies that make decisions on changes in technology based on references and reliability data. It became clear to Jack that release 1 of the new software would not be acceptable to his customers as a general rule, and that they would be waiting for release 4 or 5 before they moved to the new technology. Given this reasoning, his existing customer base becomes less of a concern in this decision; the focus shifts to how to satisfy new accounts as well as the market perception about MP and its products in general.

In my terminology, Jack recognized the crux of the issue—the focus is on the new customers, not on existing ones. This focus (Constraint 2) becomes the driving objective. He further realizes that if the company found a way to quickly satisfy new account needs (Constraint 2) and generate money quickly (Constraint 4), the company's market positioning will improve (Constraint 3).

Jack decides to delve into this deeper and build a separate layer (layer 2) for this aspect of his decision. He combines the top-level objective with this new focus on new accounts. Layer 2 of the decision is shown in Figure B-4.

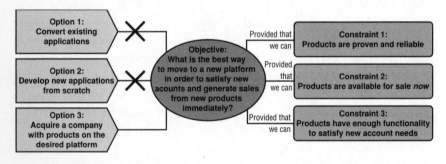

FIGURE B-4
Jack's Product Platform Layer 2 Decision Map

At that level of the decision, new constraints appear. In order to satisfy the new accounts' needs, it was urgent for MP to have software available *now* with enough functionality to satisfy the new customers' requirements. Moreover, a proven set of software was needed rather than a converted set of software that had not yet been proven.

From this perspective, neither converting existing applications (Option 1) nor rewriting them (Option 2) is a viable option anymore, simply because neither can deliver in time to satisfy the objective and constraints.

Taking all of this into account, Jack decided to abandon internal development. The company also revamps its marketing strategy— invest in the existing platform in addition to developing a new platform. This position satisfies chief information officers of existing customers. If questioned by their bosses about the future of a dying platform, they can answer the question with "MP is investing in the current platform but at the same time working on a new platform. We can switch to this platform at any time." Internally, MP continued developing the current platform so that analysts and employees continued to believe in the company and its future.

Other than separating a communications layer from the actual decision, recognizing layers in a complex decision is not easy. In my experience, the recognition usually comes when a decision maker notices during the initial decision contemplation that there are conflicts between constraints or that more depth is required in considering a particular constraint. Then, de-layering (or creating a separate decision layer for this constraint) is instrumental in making the overall decision, as Jack did in this example.

> ### Exercise
> Identify aspects of your decision that might benefit from creating a decision layer specific to them. These aspects might still be unclear or might have underlying details relevant to the overall choice.

Technique: Identifying and Formulating a New Decision Layer

Note that this technique should be used after you have completed the process of decision contemplation with the overall decision—working with your emotions, clarifying perspectives, and aligning with outcomes.

1. Focus on the specific aspect of the decision. It may be the crux question or a specific constraint. Integrate this aspect into the objective for the new decision layer. In cases when the crux question or the aspect of interest is related to two constraints, combine them into an objective for the new layer.

2. Define additional constraints for this layer using the Clarity State as needed, such as in cases where you encounter difficulties in converting concern into constraints.

3. See whether certain options are no longer valid, or create new options that are viable at this level.

4. Treat this layer as a separate decision. Work though parts of the Clarity State Decision-Making process with this layer—dealing with your emotions, reframing, and aligning with outcomes.

> **Exercise**
>
> Using the identified problematic aspects of your decision, zoom in on them by creating a separate decision layer and making a decision on it. Then zoom out to the top decision layer. Make sure that you are clear about the lessons learned and that you are surfacing to the top decision layer from the deeper layers.

As you can see, this process can be easily generalized—you can take each constraint and create a decision map where this constraint is featured as the main objective. Building layers for all constraints of the overall decision is a worthwhile exercise only in some rare cases. Usually, only one to a maximum of three constraints is important and is worth working with in this manner.

You can also imagine a situation when you can de-layer two or three times or any number of times. For example, you can build a decision map for a constraint of the original decision and then another decision map for a constraint of that layer. You can go as deep as you like. In practice, such depth is rarely necessary. One layer in addition to the top layer is usually sufficient to resolve problematic issues involved in a decision.

Breaking a decision into smaller parts is always a good practice. I found that people are confused about what parts to focus on. Paradoxically, instead of focusing on the parts that are unclear, they usually focus on the parts that are either clear or have almost no relevance to making the final choice. Listen to your gut. When you work with the overall decision, you can usually identify the parts that are vague or have details buried underneath that have relevance to the overall choice. Delve into those by creating a decision layer for this aspect of the decision. Do not leave them in the dark.

Key Point
Decision de-layering is a powerful technique that surfaces critical underlying details relevant to the overall choice.

Best Practice   If you have a complex decision, separate a communications layer and one or two other layers focused on the most critical aspects of the decision.

References

Chapter 1

1. Bossidy, Larry. Interview at Nova University. 2004.
2. Marquis de Vauvenargues. *Reflections and Maxims*. 1746.
3. Nietzsche, Friedrich. *The Antichrist*. 1888.
4. Bossidy, Larry. Interview at Nova University. 2004.
5. Janis, I. and L. Mann. *Decision Making: A Psychological Analysis of Conflict, Choice and Commitment*. New York: Free Press, 1977.
6. Festinger, L. A. *A Theory of Congnitive Dissonance*. Row Peterson, 1957.
7. Festinger, L., ed. *Conflict, Decision and Dissonance*. Stanford University Press, 1964.
8. Personal discussion. May 2003.
9. Goethe, quoted in Johan Peter Eckermann's *Conversations with Goethe*, Dec. 25, 1825.
10. Hammond, J. S., R. L. Keeney, and H. Raiffa. *Smart Choices: A Practical Guide to Making Better Decisions*. Harvard Business School Press, 1999.
11. Yates, J. F., E. S. Veinott, and A. L. Patalano. "Hard Decisions, Bad Decisions: On decision quality and decision aiding." In *Emerging Perspectives on Judgment and Decision Research*, eds. S. L. Schneider and J. Shanteau. Cambridge University Press, 2002.

Chapter 2

1. Napoleon Bonaparte. *Maxims*. 1804-15.
2. Garfield, Charles A. and Hal Zina Bennett. *Peak Performance: Mental Training Techniques of the World's Greatest Athletes.* Houghton Mifflin, 1984.
3. Childre, D. *Freeze Frame: One Minute Stress Management.* Planetary Publications: California, 1994.
4. McCraty, Rollin, William Tiller, and Mike Atkinson. "Cardiac Coherence: A New Non-invasive Measure of Autonomic System Order." *Alternative Therapies*, 1996; 2(1), 52-65.
5. Csikszentmihalyi, Mihaly. *Finding Flow: The Psychology of Engagement With Everyday Life.* Basic Books, 1997.
6. McCraty, Rollin and Mike Atkinson. "Influence of Afferent Cardiovascular Input on Cognitive Performance and Alpha Activity." In *Proceedings of the Annual Meeting of the Pavlovian Society.* Tarrytown, NY: 1999.
7. Lao Tse. *The Character of Tao.* (6th c. B.C.) 33.
8. Holmes, Oliver Wendell, Sr. *Iris, Her Book—The Professor at the Breakfast Table.* 1860.

Chapter 3

1. Napoleon Bonaparte. *Maxims*. 1804-15.
2. Browning, Elizabeth Barrett. *Casa Guidi Windows.* 1851.
3. Russo, J. E. and P. J. H. Schoemaker. *Decision Traps: The Ten Barriers to Brilliant Decision-making and How to Overcome Them.* Doubleday, 1989.
4. Hammond, J. S., R. L. Keeney, and H. Raiffa. *Smart Choices: A Practical Guide to Making Better Decisions.* Harvard Business School Press, 1999.
5. Ovid. *Ars Amatoria*, c. 10.
6. Seneca. *De Providentia.* A.D. 64.
7. Tversky, A. and D. Kahneman. 1981. "The Framing of Decisions and the Psychology of Choice." *Science* 211, 453-458.
8. Pascal. *Pensées.* 1670.

Chapter 4

1. Kawasaki, Guy. *Rules for Revolutionaries: The Capital Manifesto for Creating and Marketing New Products and Services*. Harper Collins, 2000, p. 5.

2. Langer, E. J. *Mindfulness*. Addison-Wesley, 1989.

3. Langer, E. J. *The Power of Mindful Learning*. Addison-Wesley, 1997.

4. Rahula, Walpola. *What the Buddha Taught*. Revised edition. Grove Press: July 1, 1974, p. 126.

5. Montaigne. "Of the Inconsistency of Our Actions." *Essays*. 1580-88.

6. Drucker, Peter F. *The Effective Executive*. Harper Collins, 1966, p. 113-114.

7. Emerson, Ralph Waldo. *Essays*: Second Series. 1844.

8. Virgil. *Aeneid*. 19 B.C.

Chapter 5

1. Hill, Napoleon, Bill Hartley, Arthur Morey, and Matthew Sartwell. *Principles of Personal Power: Initiative and Leadership, Imagination, Enthusiasm, Self-control (the Law of Success)*. Revised and updated edition. CA: Renaissance Books, December 1, 2002, p. 226.

2. Dickey, Thomas. The trained mind: *Total Concentration*. Time Life Books, 1988.

3. HeartMath LLC, 14700 West Park Avenue, Boulder Creek, California 95006 USA. Phone: 1-831-338-8700 or 1-800-450-9111. Fax: 1-831-338-9861.
   http://www.heartmath.com/freezeframer/index.html

4. Barrios-Choplin, B., R. McCraty, and B. Cryer. 1997. "A new approach to reducing stress and improving physical and emotional well-being at work." *Stress Medicine* 13, 193-201.

5. Lao-Tzu, Tao Teh Ching, c. 604-c. 531 B.C.

6. Vishnu-devananda, S. *The Complete Illustrated Book of Yoga*. Harmony Books, 1988.

7. Benson, Herbert. *The Relaxation Response*. Harper Collins, 2000.

8. Silva, Jose and Philip Miele. *The Silva Mind Control Method.* Simon and Schuster, 1978.

9. Gendlin, Eugene T. *Focusing.* Bantam Books, 1978.

10. Garfield, Charles A. and Hal Zina Bennett. *Peak Performance: Mental Training Techniques of the World's Greatest Athletes.* Houghton Mifflin, 1984.

11. Bacci, Ingrid. *The Art of Effortless Living: Simple Techniques for Healing Mind, Body and Spirit.* Vision Works, 2000.

12. von Ebner-Eschenbach, Marie. *Aphorisms.* 1893.

Chapter 6

1. Seneca. *De Providentia.* A.D. 64.

2. Carroll, Lewis. *Alice's Adventures in Wonderland.* Appleton, New York: 1866.

3. Boileau, Nicolas. *L'art poetique.* 1674.

4. Hammond, J. S., R. L. Keeney, and H. Raiffa. *Smart Choices: A Practical Guide to Making Better Decisions.* Harvard Business School Press, 1999.

5. Russo, J. E. and P. J. H. Schoemaker. *Winning Decisions: Getting It Right the First Time.* Currency; 1st edition, December 26, 2001.

6. Drucker, Peter F. *The Effective Executive.* Harper Collins, 1966, p. 145.

Chapter 7

1. Mann, Thomas. *The Magic Mountain.* 1924, Ch 5.

2. Donaldson, Gordon and Jay Lorsch. *Decision Making At the Top.* Basic Books, 1983.

3. Schein, Edgar H. *The Corporate Culture Survival Guide.* Jossey-Bass Publishers: San Francisco, 1999.

4. Welch, J. F. *Jack: Straight From the Gut.* Warner Business Books, 2001.

5. Colton, Charles Caleb. *Lacon.* 1825, 1.439.

6. Personal discussions. August 2003.

7. Bazerman, Max H. *Judgment in Managerial Decision Making*, 5th edition. Wiley, 2002.

Chapter 8

1. Lord Chesterfield. Letters to his son, March 9, 1748.

2. Lasarus, R. S. and B. N. Lazarus. *Passion and Reason: Making Sense of Our Emotions*. New York: Oxford University Press, 1994.

3. Richards, Mary Caroline. *Centering in Pottery, Poetry, and the Person*, revised second edition. Wesleyan University Press, May 15, 1989.

4. LeDoux, J. E. *The Emotional Brain: The Mysterious Underpinnings of Emotional Life*. New York: Simon & Schuster, 1996.

5. Damasio, A. R. *Descartes' Error: Emotion, Reason, and the Human Brain*. New York: G. P. Putnam, 1994.

6. Goleman, D. *Working With Emotional Intelligence*. New York: Bantam, 2000.

7. Mittal, Vikas and William T. Ross, Jr. "The impact of positive and negative effect and issue framing on issue interpretation and risk taking." *Organizational Behavior and Human Decision Processes* 76, no. 3 (1998): 298-324.

8. Estrada, Carlos A., Alice M. Isen, and Mark J. Young. "Positive effect facilitates integration of information and decreases anchoring in reasoning among physicians." *Organizational Behavior and Human Decision Processes* 72, no. 1 (1997): 117-135.

9. Hogarth, Robin. *Educating Intuition*. The University of Chicago Press, 2001.

10. Hammond, K. R. *Judgments Under Stress*. Oxford University Press, 2000.

11. Sarno, J. E. *Healing Back Pain: The Mind-body Connection*. Warner Books, 1991.

12. Sarno, J. E. *Mind Over Back: A Radically New Approach to the Diagnosis and Treatment of Back Pain*. Bantam, 1999.

13. Pascal. *Pensées*. 1670, 277.

Chapter 9

1. Carnegie, Dale. *How To Win Friends and Influence People*. Pocket, reissue edition. Simon & Schuster, February 15, 1990, p. 14.
2. Schellenberg, James A. *Conflict Resolution: Theory, Research, and Practice*. Albany, NY: State University of New York Press, 1996.
3. Drucker, Peter F. *The Effective Executive*. Harper Collins, 1966, p. 113-114.
4. Patton, George S. *War As I Knew It*. Houghton Mifflin Company, 1978.
5. Levine, Stewart. *The Book of Agreement: 10 Essential Elements For Getting Results You Want*. San Francisco: Berrett-Koehler, 2002.
6. Masters, Marick Francis and Robert R. Albright. *The Complete Guide To Conflict Resolution in the Workplace*. New York: AMA-COM, 2002.
7. Berglas, Steven. *The Success Syndrome: Hitting Bottom When You Reach the Top*. Plenum Publishing, 1986.
8. Braddon, Mary Elizabeth. *Lady Audley's Secret*. 1862.

Chapter 10

1. Lore, Nicholas. *The Pathfinder*. Simon & Schuster, 1998, p. 140.
2. Plous, S. *The Psychology of Judgment and Decision Making*. New York: McGraw-Hill, 1993.
3. Nietzsche, Friedrich Wilhelm. *Human, All Too Human*. 1878.
4. Hogarth, Robin. *Educating Intuition*. The University of Chicago Press, 2001.
5. Russo, J. E. and P. J. H. Schoemaker. *Decision Traps: The Ten Barriers To Brilliant Decision-making and How To Overcome Them*. Doubleday, 1989.
6. Bacon, Francis. *Of Dispatch*. 1625.

Chapter 11

1. Emerson, Ralph Waldo. "The American Scholar." Oration delivered before the Phi Beta Kappa Society, Cambridge, Massachusetts, August 31, 1837. In *Nature, Addresses and Lectures,* vol. 3 of *The Works of Ralph Waldo Emerson,* 1906.
2. Chekhov, Anton Pavlovich. *Notebooks.* 1892-1904.
3. Thoreau, Henry David. *Walden.* 1854. In *The Writings of Henry David Thoreau,* vol. 2. Houghton Mifflin, 1906.
4. Russo, J. E. and P. J. H. Schoemaker. *Decision Traps: The Ten Barriers To Brilliant Decision-making and How To Overcome Them.* Doubleday, 1989.
5. Russo, J. E. and P. J. H. Schoemaker. *Winning Decisions: Getting It Right the First Time.* Currency; 1st edition, December 26, 2001.
6. da Vinci, Leonardo. *Notebooks.* c. 1200.
7. Kahneman and Tversky. "Prospect theory: An analysis of decision under risk." *Econometrica* 47 (1979): 263-291.
8. Schwab, Charles M. *Succeeding With What You Have.* 1920.

Chapter 12

1. Drucker, Peter F. *The Effective Executive.* Harper Collins, 1966, p. 143.
2. Keller, Helen. *Optimism.* 1903.
3. Angor, Weston H. *The Logic of Intuitive Decision Making: A Research-based Approach For Top Management.* Quorum Books, 1986.
4. De Bono, Edward. *Serious Creativity: Using the Power of Lateral Thinking to Create New Ideas.* Harper Collins, 1992.
5. Plous, S. *The Psychology of Judgment and Decision Making.* New York: McGraw-Hill, 1993.
6. Bazerman, Max H. *Judgment in Managerial Decision Making,* 5th edition Wiley, 2002.
7. Belton, Valerie and Theodor J. Stewart. *Multiple Criteria Decision Analysis,* 1st edition Kluwer Academic Publishers, 2002.

8. Hogarth, Robin. *Judgment and Choice*, 2nd edition New York: John Wiley and Sons, 1987.

9. Dawes, Robyn M. *Rational Choice In An Uncertain World*. New York: Harcourt, Brace & Jovanovich, 1988.

10. Hammond, J. S., R. L. Keeney, and H. Raiffa. *Smart Choices: A Practical Guide to Making Better Decisions*. Harvard Business School Press, 1999.

11. de la Fontaine, Jean. *Fables*. 1668, fable 5.

12. Euripides. *Iphigenia in Tauris* (c. 414-12 B.C.)

13. Twain, Mark. *Pudd'nhead Wilson's Calendar*. 1894.

Chapter 13

1. Allen, James. *As a Man Thinketh*. 1890.

Appendix B

1. Gerould, Katharine Fullerton. *Modes and Morals*. 1920.

2. Marquis de Vauvenargues. *Reflections and Maxims*. 1746, 3.

3. Descartes, René. *Discourse On Method*. 1637.

Index

Why Great Leaders Don't Take Yes for an Answer
Managing for Conflict and Consensus
BY MICHAEL A. ROBERTO

Executives hear "yes" far too often. Their status and power inhibits candid dialogue. They don't hear bad news until it's too late. They get groupthink, not reality. They think they've achieved consensus, then find their decisions undermined or derailed by colleagues who never really bought in. They become increasingly isolated; even high-risk or illegal actions can begin to go unquestioned. Inevitable? Absolutely not. In this book, Harvard Business School Professor Michael Roberto shows you how to promote honest, constructive dissent and skepticism...use it to improve your decisions...and then align your entire organization to fully support the decisions you make. Drawing on his extensive research on executive decision-making, Roberto shows how to test and probe the members of your management team...discover when "yes" means "yes" and when it doesn't...and build real, deep consensus that leads to action. Along the way, Roberto offers important new insights into managing teams, mitigating risk, promoting corporate ethics through effective governance, and much more. Your organization and your executive team have immense untapped wisdom: this book will help you tap that wisdom to the fullest.

ISBN 0131454390, © 2005, 304 pp., $29.95

In the Line of Fire
How to Handle Tough Questions... When It Counts
BY JERRY WEISSMAN

You've just been asked a brutal question. How will you respond? Will you freeze? Evade? Get defensive? No way. You'll stay completely in control. You'll win them over. *In the Line of Fire* will show you how. Author Jerry Weissman began his career crafting tough questions for CBS' Mike Wallace...then became the world's #1 coach for executives planning IPO presentations with billions of dollars at stake. This book brings together everything he's learned about answering tough questions. How to prepare. How to listen. How to answer the real question. How to avoid mistakes guaranteed to lose an audience. How to get your own message across. How to control the entire interaction. You'll learn from dozens of high-profile examples, including a remarkable, blow-by-blow photo commentary on the debate answer that destroyed a Presidency. Everyone faces tough questions. Winners handle them with skill, clarity, and grace, and Jerry Weissman has spent a lifetime helping presenters do just that. Now, you can use these lessons to your advantage.

ISBN 0131855174, © 2005, 216 pp., $24.95